Why Is It So **HARD** to Get **GOOD** Schools?

Why Is It So **HARD** to Get **GOOD** Schools?

Larry Cuban

TEACHERS
COLLEGE
PRESS

Teachers College, Columbia University
New York and London

Published by Teachers College Press, 1234 Amsterdam Avenue, New York, NY 10027
Copyright © 2003 by Teachers College, Columbia University

Library of Congress Cataloging-in-Publication Data

Cuban, Larry.
    Why is it so hard to get good schools?/Larry Cuban.
p. cm.
    Includes bibliographical references and index.
     ISBN 0-8077-4294-5 (pbk.)—ISBN 0-8077-4295-3 (cloth)
     1. Public schools—United States. 2. Educational change—United
    States. I. Title.
LA217.2.C83 2003
371.01'0973—dc21 2002-027126

ISBN 0-8077-4294-5 (paper)
ISBN 0-8077-4295-3 (cloth)

Printed on acid-free paper
Manufactured in the United States of America
10 09 08 07 06 05 04 03   8 7 6 5 4 3 2 1

Contents

Acknowledgments

In the decades-long journey to make sense of "good" schools, I accumulated many debts. First, I am indebted to Arthur Levine, President of Teachers College, and Karen Zumwalt, then Dean of the College, for inviting me to give the Julius and Rosa Sachs Lectures for 2001. Their invitation pushed me to think through the issues that I had been fumbling with for many years. I appreciated very much the help of Barry Rosen and of Krystyna Davenport, who worked hard to publicize the lectures and make Milbank Chapel a welcoming venue. The Department of Organization and Leadership, chaired by Chuck Harrington, with the able assistance of Jeff Sun generously and hospitably provided me with a home away from Stanford. Marilyn Breeze, Nouri Badawi, and Amy Andruschat answered all of my questions, even the trivial ones, and provided me essential support for my writing, the lectures, and my course. The students I taught, yes, in the "good" schools course, and my TC faculty colleagues, particularly Dorothy Shipps, David Hansen, Tom Sobol, Bob Monson, Hank Levin, Clifford Hill, and Anna Neumann, were both stimulating and gracious. I could ask for no more during a semester marked forever by September 11th.

Beyond Teachers College, I was blessed with friends who made that autumn in New York and my work on these lectures a special time for me. I want to thank Joel Westheimer for those lovely bike rides and wide-ranging conversations in Central Park, along the Hudson River, in Putnam County and central New Jersey, and out to Coney Island. I appreciated very much the friendship that he, Barbara, Michal, and his mother, Ruth, extended to me during my 4 months in the city. Renewing a friendship with Sam Bryan and his wife, Amy Scott, and with Nancy Lester, a former colleague at Stanford now at Medgar Evers College, added to my delight at being in New York.

I also want to thank my wife, Barbara, for her many trips to New York while managing a lively private practice in Palo Alto. Those fun-filled weekends exhilarated me even if the walks all over Manhattan gave me sore feet. Finally, both Barbara and I thank Rita Charon and Bernard Gross for their many acts of friendship, especially when we most needed it.

Larry Cuban
April 2002

Why Is It So
HARD
to Get
GOOD
Schools?

Introduction

These lectures tie together different strands of my life and work over the last half-century. My experience as a teacher, beginning in McKeesport, Pennsylvania (1955), then on to Cleveland, Ohio (1956–1963) and Washington, DC (1963–1972), forged my later thinking as a superintendent (1974–1981) and researcher (1981–2001). Returning briefly to the classroom in the 1980s and 1990s further framed my thinking about teacher education, curriculum, school administration, and the messy linkages between educational policy and classroom practice.

Two hard-earned truths about teaching have governed my thinking for decades. First, I know from both experience and research that the teacher is at the heart of student learning and school improvement by virtue of being the classroom authority and gatekeeper for change. Thus, the preparation, induction, and career development of teachers remain the Archimedean lever for both short- and long-term improvement of public schools.

A second truth is anchored in the first. Given the high and unmet expectations for schools in this country—schooling is popularly viewed as the solvent for national social ills and an individual escalator to social and financial success—both administrators and policymakers, seeking improvement in students' performance, view teachers, paradoxically, as both the problem and the solution to school defects. Parlaying these contradiction-filled truths into a coherent approach to teaching, administering schools, and making sensible policies for urban schools has driven much of my writing for scholars and practitioners. All of this provides some background for my work on "good" schools. [1]

I put "good" in quotation marks because it is obviously not a technical term but a common one that is in everyday use by top policymakers, educators, business leaders, parents, and taxpayers. A "good" school also can be described as "great," "excellent," "first-rate," or by other similar terms. Common as these terms are, there is no agreed-on meaning to the word or phrases. Moreover, the words and phrases encompass many notions of "goodness" including Effective Schools, Core Knowledge Schools, Accelerated Schools, Coalition of Essential Schools, Success for All Schools, and dozens of other designs for a "good" school.

As ambiguous as the phrase "good" schools is, I have wrestled with the concept for many years. I can date the beginning of these lectures back to 1968. In January of that year, I had accepted a post at the U.S. Commission on Civil Rights (USCCR) as Director of their Race and Education unit. I was then teaching social studies (including a course on Negro History) at Roosevelt High School in Washington, DC. I didn't want to leave my students until the end of the school year so I split my time between teaching two morning classes at the high school and going downtown to work afternoons in the USCCR building. Following the April 1968 assassination of Martin Luther King, Jr., rioters had destroyed much of 14th Street, a block away from my school. During the disturbances, our school was closed; students and teachers were evacuated. In June, as planned, I left Roosevelt High School to work fulltime at the commission.

The primary goal of the U.S. Commission on Civil Rights was to advance racial integration in every aspect of American life, and I was committed to that mission. We lived in one of the few intentionally and sustained integrated neighborhoods in Washington, DC—a school district that had become largely re-segregated within a decade of the *Bolling v. Sharpe* (1955) decision declaring segregated schools unconstitutional in the District of Columbia. Our children walked to their nearby school.

In the wake of the 1968 riots in Washington and elsewhere, however, racial turmoil disturbed relations among the integrated staff at the commission and raised serious issues about the worth of integration in improving schools, particularly in cities. In most big cities across the nation, restrictive housing policies produced de facto segregated school systems with large majorities of poor black and Latino students. High dropout rates, low test scores, and a culture of academic failure permeated most—but not all—urban schools.

At the commission, a few of us had pointed out that racially isolated schools in Detroit, Newark, Atlanta, and similarly situated cities were hardly candidates for district-wide integration unless city-suburb mergers occurred and the U.S. Supreme Court declared cross-district consolidation of schools constitutional. While such court cases were wending their way to the U.S. Supreme Court, a few of us thought that improving ghetto schools should be explored. We offered as evidence examples of "good" ghetto schools, that is, poor all-black elementary schools where students kept pace with or outscored nonpoor, mostly white elementary schools on reading and math standardized achievement tests.

The leadership of the USCCR, at that time, saw such proposals as antithetical to its mandate to push for integrated education. Turnover in the leadership, continuing racial friction, and disputes over educational direction led to my leaving the commission. But the idea of "good" ghetto schools resurfaced a few years later when I became superintendent of the Arlington (Virginia) public schools.

Arlington's school population was getting smaller and nonwhite. A decline in overall enrollment with increasing percentages of Asian and Latino immigrants entering the schools in the mid-1970s added to the African-American residents who had been in the county since the end of the Civil War. These demographic changes substantially altered the composition of the district's schools. Struggles over desegregation of all-black schools in the district had been largely settled by 1972 through the establishment of magnet and alternative schools. Nonetheless, children of newcomers filled schools in the southern and central parts of the district where the black population was located. These rising proportions of minorities in the Arlington schools alarmed the white majority, triggering fears of a decline in the quality of schooling.

The school board that appointed me in 1974 was determined to maintain the high quality of schooling—then interpreted as stability in state test scores—in light of the changing school population and the appearance of mostly minority schools. For 7 years, the board and I worked hard at establishing clear and explicit academic goals, creating accountability mechanisms, and mandating processes that spurred teachers and principals not only to expect high performance in the one-third of the schools that were largely minority but also to reconfigure their schedules and programs to produce the desired outcomes, including higher test scores.

By the late 1970s, the emerging "Effective Schools" movement and the work of Ron Edmonds created a rhetoric of high expectations ("all children can learn") for urban schools and a template of "effective" practices (clear goals, high academic standards, raised expectations for students achieving, frequent assessment, etc.). Effective Schools reformers assembled instances where poor children scored well on state and national tests and publicized them. The national movement helped our efforts in Arlington. I brought Ron Edmonds to Arlington in 1980 to reinforce the message that largely minority schools with high percentages of low-income students can be "good." By the end of my tenure in the district, we published annual reports of school-by-school student performance on various measures broken out by ethnic and racial background. Scores on state-mandated tests had risen in all elementary schools but had stalled at the secondary level. The gap between minority and white test scores remained although there were signs that it might be closing.

I left the superintendency in 1981 and came to Stanford to teach and write. One of the courses that I offered was "Research, Policy, and Practice of Effective Schools." Between 1981 and 2001, I taught the course 12 times. In each instance, the course changed as my students and I came to grips with the literature, national school reforms, and the changing nature of what was construed as "effective."

For example, Ron Edmonds and other Effective Schools researchers and reformers concentrated on ghetto schools, mostly elementary ones. By the late 1980s, however, "effective" programs aimed solely at urban schools had spread to suburban and rural districts for both elementary and secondary schools. By then, Title I of the Elementary and Secondary Education Act required schools to embrace Effective Schools programs. In 1989, President George Bush convened the nation's governors and established six national goals, later expanded to eight by President Bill Clinton. In the early 1990s, the goals of high academic standards and improved academic achievement, and a slogan of the Effective Schools movement—"all children can learn"— had become appropriated by business leaders, public officials, parents, and educators and transformed into a national effort for educational uplift. What was once called "effective" and aimed primarily at urban elementary schools had now become an intense national quest for creating uniform "good" schools. The course I taught mirrored those changes. By the early 1990s, I had renamed the Effective Schools course: "Good Schools: Research, Policy, and Practice."

The journey from searching for "good" ghetto schools in 1968 at the U.S. Commission on Civil Rights to pressing principals and teachers in largely low-income, minority schools in Arlington during the 1970s to expect more of their students to, finally, teaching and writing about "good" schools at Stanford is the direct route I traveled to Teachers College, Columbia University, in 2001.

Yet recounting how I came to "good" schools as a topic for these lectures should not obscure the quarter-century I spent in classrooms and administrative offices. Those experiences molded my thinking about the centrality of teaching to substantial and lasting school improvement and forced me into helping policymakers, practitioners, and researchers come to grips with the stubborn paradox of viewing teachers as both the problem and the solution in creating "good" schools.

In the three lectures that follow—Chapters 1, 2, and 3—readers will find instances where my background as a practitioner becomes foreground. That is intentional because I believe that both experience-produced knowledge and research-produced knowledge are essential to the practice of schooling and its improvement. In the following chapters, I have largely retained the language of each lecture rather than converting the spoken word into the printed word. Additions, deletions, or amendments to a lecture occurred because of comments from those who attended the lectures, errors of facts that I or a colleague discovered, or insights gained from subsequent research. None of these changes substantially altered the argument that unfolds in these lectures.

1

Why Have American Public Schools Become an Arm of the Economy?

> *There is hardly any work we can do or any expenditures we can make that will yield so large a return to our industries as would come from the establishment of educational institutions which would give us skilled hands and trained minds for the conduct of our industries and our commerce.*
> —Theodore Search, President of the National Association of Manufacturers, 1898[1]

> *Education isn't just a social concern, it's a major economic issue. If our students can't compete today, how will our companies compete tomorrow? In an age when a knowledgeable work force is a nation's most important resource, American students rank last internationally in calculus and next to last in algebra.*
> —John Akers, chairman of IBM, 1991[2]

The above quotations illustrate the major claim that I make in this first lecture. At two separate points in the past, the end of the 19th century and then again at the end of the 20th century, business-led coalitions forged political alliances among public officials, union leaders, educators, and community activists to draft public schools into preparing students for skilled jobs. In those two instances, training students for the ever-changing work-

place has overwhelmed the literacy, civic, and moral goals that have historically guided public education. Consequently, age-graded schools have
become an arm of the national economy. "Good jobs," President George W.
Bush said, "begin with good schools." In getting students ready for an information-based workplace, American schools now concentrate on rigorously
preparing all students for college, thus perpetuating one ideological version
of a "good" school. How and why did this happen?[3]

Before answering the question, let me step back for a moment to give
you an overview of all three lectures so you will get a sense of the direction I will be traveling. In these lectures, I will argue that a business-
inspired version of a "good" school has converged with popular views of
what is a "good" school to create an educational orthodoxy of a one-best-
school for all American children. I claim that this market-driven ideology
about what constitutes a "good" school undermines tax-supported public
education. The official version of a "good" school is bad for education
because, like a prehistoric insect trapped in amber, it freezes a traditional
curriculum and instruction, hardens a century-old age-graded school
organization, and perpetuates the myth of a one-best-school.

As bad as that is for public schools, there is more. The current orthodoxy of a "good" school ignores the history of many "good" schools that
has marked American public and private education for almost 2 centuries
and neglects the fundamental purpose of public schools of transforming
children into civic-minded, independent-thinking, and socially responsible adults committed to both the common good and engaging in productive work. In my final lecture I will offer alternative directions for age-
graded public schools and teaching that are more consistent with the
central purpose of public schools in a democracy.

With this brief overview of the three lectures, I now turn to how and why
business leaders have formed coalitions twice in the past century to reform
public schools and the harmful consequences of that involvement.

In the 1880s and in the 1980s, business-led reformers' coalitions, fearing
foreign competition in carving out a large share of the global market, wanted public schools to train an efficient workforce that would give American
products an edge in international trade, and ultimately fuel domestic prosperity. In both cases, these reformers believed that students lacked work-
related skills and that age-graded schools should be modeled after the cor-
poration and the marketplace. In these two periods of reform, business
involvement in U.S. public schools was influential in changing school goals,
governance, management, and curriculum. But this involvement seldom
altered dominant classroom practices.

This may sound surprising because corporate leaders were and are
committed to enhancing their firms' profits, their "bottom line." Applied

to age-graded schools, the bottom line to business-minded reformers in the early 20th century meant better teaching and learning. Yet in classrooms, reformers have had little influence. Now, in the early 21st century, business leaders, educators, and public officials no longer define the bottom line as better teaching and learning; the bottom line is securing higher test scores. New York City Chancellor Harold Levy crisply expressed this view.

> That's the bottom line. Business has profit and loss. The school system has students and ... there is nothing more important than our getting the children up to the levels of reading and math so that they can get through these exams and go on to successful careers. That's what this system is about. The minute we take our eyes off that we begin doing something wrong.[4]

Market-inspired reformers care little about transforming classroom practices; they care a lot about raising test scores. Major influence on school goals, management, and governance and minor impact on the educational bottom line is a puzzle I will return to later in the lecture.

In elaborating my claim about these influences, I must be clear as to what I mean by such terms as "business involvement," "reform," and the "age-graded school."

Business interest in schools has largely involved private individuals and groups drawn from a variety of large, middle-sized, and small businesses. There is no monolithic business community (nor has there been) such as "Big Business" that has shaped and steered U.S. public schools. Of course, corporate elites have existed (and continue to exist) in the United States. And, yes, private businesses are highly organized and possess resources that many other groups lack. But the diversity of businesses from multinational Fortune 500 companies to regional and national business associations to local Chambers of Commerce involved in so many school activities is far more apparent than a corporate elite that has single-mindedly engineered changes in U.S. schools.[5]

Over the past century, business firms have started private schools, helped to improve school management, donated cash and equipment, and persuaded children, teachers, and parents of the importance of getting skills to succeed in a market economy. In the policy arena, business leaders formed coalitions of like-minded executives to lobby state and federal legislators to enact favorite education bills. These alliances believed that more and better schooling would bolster worker skills and strengthen the economy while building civic-minded graduates and helping individuals earn decent salaries.[6]

By "school reform" I refer to solutions to problems. Public school critics identify problems that must be solved. Reformers design solutions and mobilize coalitions to make changes happen. The two examples of reforms as solutions to problems that I will use are vocational education in the late 19th century and the late 20th century standards-driven testing and account-ability movement. Both reforms took for granted the age-graded school, an earlier solution to the problem of inefficient rural one-room schools.

As post–Civil War America slowly evolved into an urban industrial economy, the age-graded school, an import from Prussia, promised far more efficient public schooling to fit a manufacturing-based economy than the prevailing one-room schools. Between 1840 and 1920, cities adopted the innovation of the age-graded school at all levels, eventually making virtual museums of one-room schools.

The age-graded school had a principal in charge of a multi-classroom building where each teacher had a separate room with children sorted by age into first, second, and subsequent grades. Each classroom had to complete a portion of the prescribed curriculum or subject within 30 or so weeks. Those students who could demonstrate that they learned the content and skills were promoted; those who could not repeated the year or subject. This school organization sharply focused on teachers covering particular content and skills within a prescribed time shaped how teachers taught in their sep-arate classrooms.[7]

BUSINESS-LED SCHOOL REFORM

With these clarifications in mind, I turn the historical clock back to the 1880s to elaborate the claim that I made about business involvement in reforming schools. I begin with the earlier period and then move the clock forward to the late 20th century.

1880s–1930s

In the 1880s and 1890s, top industrialists expressed strong fears that U.S. products were losing ground to British and German ones. When American business leaders traveled to Germany to determine how the country had so quickly become a world trade rival to Great Britain, they often pointed to German technical schools' graduating highly skilled workers.

In the years prior to World War I, a progressive alliance evolved among American business leaders, top public officials, unions, and educators that promoted new courses and nontraditional forms of teaching such as stu-dent-made projects. Eventually educational reformers championing novel courses in woodworking, metal shops, and drawing and progressive teaching practices merged with union leaders who wanted industrial arts courses in public rather than in private employer-run schools. Both groups joined business-minded reformers eager to strengthen the U.S. share of international trade by drafting schools into a race to end the industrial-skills deficit among American students. By 1910 the merger was complete and had become the vocational education movement.[8]

Occasional voices objected to the rush toward training students for the workplace. New York City Superintendent William Maxwell attacked manufacturers:

> They had practically abandoned the apprenticeship system of training workmen. No longer training their own mechanics, they have found it difficult to obtain a sufficient supply of skillful artisans, unless they import them from Europe at great expense. Out of this dilemma the exit was obvious—persuade the State to assume the burden.... And, as a first step to secure their ends, they and their agents in unmeasured terms denounced the public schools as behind ...as inefficient, as lacking in public spirit. And why? Because the public schools are not training artisans—are not doing the work that has been done by employers of labor for thousands of years.[9]

Less accusatory but making a similar point of business leaders turning to public schools to meet their labor needs, social reformer Jane Addams said:

> The business man has, of course, not said to himself: "I will have the public school train office boys and clerks for me, so that I may have them cheap," but he thought, and sometimes said, "Teach the children to write legibly, and to figure accurately and quickly: to acquire the habits of punctuality and order; to be prompt to obey, and not question why; and you will fit them to make their way in the world as I have made mine!" [10]

Reformers rejected such criticisms.

In 1917, this vocational education coalition succeeded in securing for the first time federal funding for industrial courses in American schools. By 1930, most urban high schools had added to their curriculum a vocational track with federally funded courses. Many cities had separate public vocational schools. Instruction in these classes was distinctly different from that in academic courses. For the most part, teachers had students actively involved in designing, repairing, and completing real-life work projects that had cash value outside of school.[11]

Nor was this introduction of vocational education into U.S. schools as a reform the only influence that business-inspired ideas and practices had on schooling. Even while condemning industrialists as greedy robber barons for their shabby business practices, progressive reformers admired corporate leaders for their stress on scientific efficiency and professional management. In San Francisco, for example, a progressive coalition of the Chamber of

Commerce, the Merchants Association, the Real Estate Board, and the City Federation of Women's Clubs campaigned to end the practice of electing a superintendent of schools. They believed that professional educators should run schools on business principles and not campaign for votes.[12]

Progressive reformers detested the large, politically appointed school boards of 50 to 100 members who gave friends and relatives district jobs and took company bribes to buy their textbooks. Reformers wanted to copy smaller and more efficient corporate boards that hired professionally trained managers. By 1930, these reformers had converted most school boards into businesslike operations with modern managerial practices divorced from partisan politics.[13]

Thus, between 1880 and 1930, major domestic economic changes and U.S. expansion into world trade shaped public schooling. Corporate leaders and business associations viewed age-graded schools as crucial in producing a trained workforce that would strengthen American international competitiveness. Alliances between business and civic officials succeeded in gaining federal support for vocational courses and guidance in secondary schools.

Moreover, progressive reformers had adopted the corporate model of efficient school governance. They moved from large, politically appointed school boards and untrained administrators to small elected boards led by business and civic-minded lay people who hired professionally trained experts to run their schools. This pattern continued into the late 20th century, when the second major surge of business involvement in schools occurred.

1980s–2000

Beginning in the mid-1970s, the decline of U.S. workplace productivity, rising unemployment, and losses in market share to Japanese and German products led corporate leaders and public officials to locate reasons for the poor performance of the American economy. Within a few years, employer criticism of high school graduates unprepared for the workplace, low test scores, violence in urban schools, and the flight of white middle-class families from cities to suburbs fixed blame on American public schools. Corporate and public officials organized political-action groups called Business Roundtables to attack the problem of unskilled workers and ineffective schools.[14]

By 1983, a president-appointed commission had produced an assessment of public schools in *A Nation at Risk*. This report crystallized the growing sense of unease with public schooling in the business community by linking mediocre student performance on national and international tests to low worker productivity and the United States' mediocre economic performance in the global marketplace.[15]

After the publication of *A Nation at Risk*, state after state increased high school graduation requirements, lengthened the school year, and added tests for students to take. In urban schools, academics and practitioners had already mobilized an Effective Schools movement that concentrated on raising students' academic achievement. The business-inspired national Commission on the Skills of the American Workplace published its highly influential report, *America's Choice: High Skills or Low Wages*. In an unprecedented act in 1989, President George Bush convened the 50 governors to discuss education. They called for six national goals (later expanded to eight by President Clinton), one of which called for American students to rank first on international tests in math and science by the year 2000. Business leaders drawn from all segments of the private sector and political leaders of both parties endorsed the creation of the National Skills Standards Board as part of the Goals 2000 legislation and, later, during the Clinton administration, endorsed the School-to-Work Opportunities Partnership Act. All of these efforts were "an easy sell," according to one top U.S. Department of Education official, because staff in each administration told business leaders that "our agenda is your agenda."[16]

What drove this alliance of public officials, corporate leaders, and educators were key, but often unstated, assumptions:

- They assumed that excessive bureaucracy in districts and a lack of accountability had lowered academic standards (particularly in math and science), undermined rigorous teaching, and graduated students mismatched to the skill demands of an information-based workplace.
- They assumed that better management, high academic standards, increased competition among schools for students, and clear incentives and penalties would improve teaching and learning and end the skills mismatch.
- They assumed that the best measures of improved teaching and learning were higher standardized test scores.
- Finally, they assumed that higher test scores would mean that future employees would perform better in the workplace.[17]

Acting on these core beliefs, presidents, governors, and corporate leaders promoted ways to solve the problem of low academic performance. Essentially, reformers in the 1980s and 1990s "borrow[ed] from the corporate closet" and copied what successful businesses have done. Top corporate leaders and Business Roundtables claimed that market-sensitive strategies had worked for Ford Motor Company, IBM, General Electric, Hewlett-Packard, and scores of other firms in earning high dividends for their shareholders. These strategies could be applied to schools. The corporate formula for success was crisp.[18]

- Set clear goals and high standards for employees.
- Restructure operations so that managers and employees who actually make the product decide what to do. Then hold those managers and employees responsible for product quality.
- Reward those who meet or exceed their goals. Shame or punish those who fail. [19]

But how does this corporate model of success fit nearly 15,000 school boards where lay citizens, not experts, make policy in public sessions, tell professionals what they must do, seek broader civic purposes than profit-taking, and declare no dividend to stockholders at the end of the fiscal quarter? Despite these substantial differences between public school governance and businesses, top corporate leaders, scores of governors, and U.S. Presidents have laid out the steps for educators to follow:

- Establish rigorous academic standards that all students must meet.
- Test students often.
- Reward those staff members, students, and schools that meet standards; shame and punish those that don't.
- Secure sharp managers who concentrate on raising academic achievement and trimming bureaucracies.
- Tell parents and taxpayers exactly how their children and schools perform on tests by issuing periodic report cards.
- Let parents choose which schools their children will attend.

This market-based prescription for public school improvement crossed political party lines. Since the early 1980s, Democratic and Republican state governors and legislatures have moved swiftly to establish curricular standards, impose tests, and hold teachers and administrators responsible for student outcomes with such devices as cash payments and taking over failing schools and districts.[20]

Giving parents choices in selecting their children's schools has also expanded dramatically in recent years. Private companies now run public schools. There are over 2,100 independent charter schools. There are also a handful of state-designed experiments that give vouchers or checks to parents who can use them in private schools. In short, the corporate model of market competition, choice, and accountability has been largely copied by states and districts and has been adopted as a de facto national policy.[21]

The wholesale application of a business model for success is only part of the pervasive influence that the private sector has had on public schools. Managerial strategies derived from command-and-control business firms include renaming superintendents "CEOs" and their deputies, "chief operating officers" and "chief academic officers." Contracting school functions to private firms and importing managerial innovations such as Total Quality Management from the private sector are common. Schools now use information technology for communication, compiling data for decision-making, and supporting teaching and learning. In less than two decades the number of students per computer has dropped from over 125 in the early 1980s to about 5 last year. Also, commercialization of curriculum and instruction has occurred. Channel 1 television, which is now in one-quarter of all high schools, displays ads for all students to watch in their 12-minute programs in exchange for supplying free equipment; schools receive funds for signing exclusive contracts to sell soft drinks and advertising space in schools.[22]

Missing from this inventory of business influences is teaching and learning. Have business approaches altered what routinely occurs in classrooms? Apart from the commercialization of some instructional materials, Channel 1 television, and classroom computers, it is hard to determine whether teachers now teach differently than they did before the late 1970s when the surge of private-sector involvement began its sweep across America's public schools.

The few studies that have been done on classroom teaching and learning before and after serious business involvement confirm the persistence of teacher-centered instruction, especially in secondary schools but less apparent in the lower grades. If anything, the impact of standards-based performance and accountability has weakened progressive teaching practices while hardening traditional teaching patterns. A progressive movement for portfolios, project-based teaching, performance-based assessment, and other student-centered approaches that had blossomed in the mid-1980s until the early 1990s, for example, has since shriveled under the pressure for higher test scores.[23]

As a consequence of almost a quarter-century of business involvement through philanthropy, partnerships, and imitation of corporate practices, public schools have become more businesslike in governance and management, and in offering parents choices of schools.

A 1999 manifesto on teachers sponsored by the Thomas B. Fordham Foundation and signed by, among others, William Bennett, Diane Ravitch, and E.D. Hirsch applauded this approach to school improvement.

> The good news is that America is beginning to adopt a powerful, commonsensical strategy for school reform. It is the same approach that almost every successful modern enterprise has adopted to boost performance and productivity: set high standards for results to be achieved, identify clear indicators to measure progress toward those results, and be flexible and pluralistic about the means to reach those results. [24]

Yet as actual choice of schools was broadened, the type of schooling children receive has narrowed considerably. To ensure that American schools produce skilled graduates ready to enter computerized workplaces, a uniform curriculum and instruction geared to preparing all children to attend college has emerged in cities and suburbs. It is a schooling in which students are expected to listen to their teachers, do their homework, get high grades, and score well on standardized tests. It is a schooling in which administrators, teachers, and students are held responsible for performing better than they did the previous year.

In the past quarter-century, then, the alliance of business leaders, public officials, and educators has taken the traditional age-graded public school and made it into a standardized experience for American students. Including the classroom. The bottom line, borrowed from business vocabulary, means better test scores. This stress on scores has glamorized traditional instructional practices while jinxing progressive ones. In effect, one model of a "good' school and one type of "good" teaching has hardened a political orthodoxy geared to making public schools into an arm of the economy.

ASSESSING BUSINESS-INSPIRED REFORM

Here, then, are two distinct periods, a century apart, in which coalitions of business leaders, unionists, public officials, and educators believing that high school graduates were unequipped for the workplace reshaped the goals, curriculum, governance, and management of U.S. public schools.

And what of the classroom? In the closing decades of the 19th century, progressive reformers, including business leaders, established the kindergarten, manual arts and vocational education curricula, the junior high school, and the comprehensive high school to cope with differences among students in their motivation, interests, social backgrounds, and academic aptitude. Throughout most of the 20th century, progressive teaching practices such as the project method and connecting curriculum to the real world seeped into elementary school classrooms. But within most secondary classrooms, teacher-centered—or what many progressives sneeringly called "traditional" practices—continued to dominate the student's day. Except for the kindergarten, junior high school, and vocational courses, corporate-influenced progressive reform over a century ago hardly touched most classrooms.[25]

A century later, the U.S. economy is anchored not in manufacturing but in the creation and distribution of information and services. Corporate leaders now see academic courses as essential for 21st-century jobs. English, history, literature, math, science, and foreign languages—once considered liberal arts courses—are now viewed by employers as vocational subjects since they equip students with the proper attitudes and skills needed in an information-based workplace. As one writer who co-authored books on public schools with CEOs from Xerox, IBM, and Proctor and Gamble put it, a solid academic education gives graduates "the capacity to solve problems, the ability to work with different people in different settings, the capacity to continue learning on the job, the ability to work in teams, honesty, punctuality, [and] reliability."[26]

Unsurprisingly, business-led coalitions have pressed states and districts for higher academic standards, test-score improvement, and accountability, all measures aimed at graduating students with high school and college credentials signaling employers that young people have acquired the necessary workplace attitudes and skills. But these reforms also negatively affected those classrooms where progressive teaching practices had been well established for decades. [27]

By the late 1990s, for example, once progressive kindergartens, middle schools, vocational education leaders and academic teachers who sought deeper student understanding have altered their practices. Kindergartens have become increasingly boot camps for the first grade; middle schools have become staging grounds for rigorous high school courses; and there has been a steady decline in traditional vocational education courses as high schools have become increasingly college preparatory and test-driven. If anything, the age-graded school with its time schedules, curriculum divided by grades, frequent tests, annual promotions, and teacher-centered practices has been polished and buffed up for the 21st century.[28]

Note that many of those historic progressive practices in kindergartens, middle schools, and vocational courses now being shunned were the very ones hailed by an earlier generation of business-minded reformers. [29]

These ironic consequences hint at the limits of business involvement in schools. Why have business-led coalitions in the past century had so little success in transforming classroom practices yet now have frozen in place traditional forms of school organization and teaching?

The answer to the question is twofold: The political arena where educational goals and policies are enacted is one that business leaders influence but hardly control. Second, business-inspired alliances seldom understand or even consider the powerful linkage between the age-graded school and classroom practices. I take up each part of the answer to define the limits of business involvement in schools.[30]

Elected school boards walk a political tightrope between their view of appropriate goals and practices and being responsive to shifts in public opinion and active lobbying by well-organized groups, including business leaders. Moreover, in state legislatures and the U.S. Congress, business groups have become active players in pressing for school reform. Even though those corporate lobbies are far better funded than nonprofit and smaller interest groups, they still must compete with one another in local, state, and federal forums to champion their favorite innovations. Inside and outside school systems, then, politics have limited business influence.[31]

Examples from the decades before World War I include union leaders' successfully resisting business initiatives to establish private vocational schools that would graduate workers trained to take jobs in local companies. Union leaders then wanted a public education that prepared workers' children to be citizens first and workers second, especially if those vocational school graduates might eventually become strikebreakers.[32]

A contemporary example of how conflicting interests limit business influence occurred in the early 1990s. In Charlotte, North Carolina, the IBM CEO shook hands with the district superintendent and agreed to contribute $2 million for four new high-tech schools to be built on land adjacent to the company. The handshake committed the superintendent to reserve a substantial portion of school space for children of IBM employees. When parents in other parts of the district realized that they would not be able to apply for the available seats in the new schools, they were outraged and protested to the school board.

IBM soon found out that the elected school board, not the superintendent, negotiates deals. Now the IBM executives, like any private or public group, would have to speak to school board members, attend public hearings, and mobilize support for their plan. Months of public controversy over the agreement led to an embarrassed and chastened IBM renegotiating a contract with the school board.

IBM executives would have nodded in agreement with the observation about public schools that New York City Chancellor Harold Levy—himself a corporate lawyer—had made: "It is not a command-and-control system," Levy said. "There are all kinds of shifting coalitions that a Chancellor needs for a support network and, in that sense, it is profoundly different from the corporate world."[33]

Nor does command-and-control extend into the classroom. Recall the puzzle I mentioned earlier about how reshaping the educational bottom line has escaped business leaders. A century ago, for example, popular support for major reforms in school governance, curriculum, and instruction made business leaders into educational progressives. In those decades, corporate leaders, unionists, and public officials promoted classroom practices in which students worked with both their heads and their hands on actual projects rather than copying lessons from textbooks and listening to teachers. They wanted to transform classroom teaching and learning. That coalition a century ago succeeded in adding vocational education to the curriculum. But the progressive teaching practices they endorsed hardly altered mainstream academic teaching practices within the age-graded school.

Now, a century later, a similar coalition says that more and tougher academic subjects equip graduates with essential workplace skills and attitudes suitable for an information-based economy. Since the mid-1980s, reformers have called for and got a uniform academic curriculum stripped of vocational courses. Reformers have triumphed in getting more tests so that now teachers, using traditional classroom practices, spend much time preparing students for tests and college admissions.[34]

What business-minded reformers wanted for state and local curriculum, tests, and accountability has largely been achieved at the cost of freezing school organization and teaching practices that an earlier generation of business-led reformers had severely criticized. The bottom line has shifted from better teaching and learning to higher test scores. Now, only one kind of "good" district, only one kind of "good" school, and only one kind of "good" teaching has become politically correct.

According to this ideology, a "good" district holds principals and teachers accountable for raising academic achievement. A "good" school is age-graded, where all students move from one level to another after 36 weeks. A "good" school is one in which teachers rely on textbooks, give lots of homework, and test students often to see if they are learning the prescribed content and skills. In a "good" school, students take rigorous subjects, master content, score well on annual standardized tests, and enter college.

I do not want to leave the impression that the success of this current reform coalition in creating a one-best-kind "good" school has foisted an unpopular view on unaware or unwilling parents and taxpayers. On the contrary, the consensus among business leaders, policymakers, teachers' unions, and civic groups of what constitutes a "good" school has converged with a similar view of schooling that many—but not all—parents and taxpayers have held for decades.

In reviewing public opinion polls since the 1940s, I have found time and again that respondents wanted safe public schools that ensured basic literacy, taught respect for authority, and instilled proper behavior in children. They also wanted age-graded schools to monitor student academic achievement and give parents reports on how their children compare with others, both locally and nationally. Repeatedly, Americans have told pollsters that they wanted their schools to prepare graduates to go on to college. For the past two decades, corporate executives and top public officials were preaching sermons about educating children that most—but not all—parents and taxpayers already believed.[35]

CONCLUSIONS

I have argued that corporate involvement in U.S. public schools, driven by a deep belief in strong schools' producing a strong economy, has been sustained and influential in twice changing goals, governance, management, and curriculum but limited in altering dominant classroom practices. I believe I have evidence from two different periods to make my claim credible. So what?

Any answer to the "so what?" question should reexamine the theory, strategies, and assumptions that drove business-minded reformers to build alliances with public officials, union leaders, educators, and ultimately with most parents and taxpayers. For example, what's so bad about focusing on preparing students for a very different workplace than their parents experienced? After all, shouldn't students come to appreciate the importance of productive labor? Of course they should. Keep in mind, however, that this goal and the policies that flow from it are no more, no less, than a value; policies that have made schools an arm of the economy twice have had very little evidence to justify the position other than that particular interest groups fought for the value. And the primacy of preparation for the workplace, the transforming of academic subjects like English, history, science, and math—heretofore considered the liberal arts—into virtual vocational subjects, has seriously distorted the historical goals that have driven public schools for well over a century.

David Labaree has nicely summarized the conflicting and oscillating tensions among public school goals. The original and abiding goal of all tax-supported public schools was democratic equality. Giving American children equal access to schooling and literacy would build citizens who could serve on juries, govern communities, and make the right judgment as voters in local, state, and national elections. Reformers accepted the wisdom of this civic goal throughout most of the 19th century.[36]

By the end of 19th century, however, the social-efficiency goal, that is, preparing students to take their place in an industrialized, socially stratified nation as both workers and well-adjusted citizens, became the primary purpose, pushing aside the civic goal. Vocational education and school stratification of students became by-products of this purpose.

Also becoming clear in the early 20th century was the fact that education was becoming an individual's ticket to a better-paid, financially secure job. The social-mobility goal for poor and lower-middle-class families transformed the age-graded public school into a personal escalator for their sons and daughters to rise into a higher social class. Education had become a private rather than a public good.

By the end of the 20th century, the tensions and interactions between these competing goals had become realigned as a consequence of business-inspired reform coalitions. What emerged as the primary goal for public schools is preparation for college, the workplace, and personal success. Trailing far behind is the goal of building citizens. Of course, all of the jostling among goals and realigning of priorities has influenced the curriculum, school organization, management, and governance of schools.[37]

Knowing the history of these conflicting goals makes it possible to ask informed questions. For example: Has the goal of social efficiency, that is, the strategies and tools borrowed from the corporate closet to make schools produce skilled graduates, worked? Can the past decade of unbroken economic prosperity in the United States be attributed to improved schools producing trained graduates who have helped companies compete in the global economy? Few economists or corporate leaders would answer yes to these questions because persuasive evidence to make such claims is unavailable.

In effect, national and state leaders have adopted, without challenge, the following assumptions as truths:

- They assumed that better management, rigorous academic standards, increased competition among schools for students, and incentives and penalties would produce better teaching and learning and higher test scores. No substantial evidence exists to support this assumption.[38]
- They assumed that the best measures of improved teaching and learning are taking more academic subjects, scoring well on standardized tests, securing credentials, and moving into skilled jobs. Yet very little evidence exists to show whether students who take math and science courses or who score well on standardized achievement tests do well in entry-level jobs or in college.[39]
- They assumed that penalties and rewards get teachers to teach better and students to learn more. That teachers now spend more

time preparing students for tests, use familiar teaching practices, and produce higher test scores hardly constitutes better teaching or student learning.

The profound gap between these assumptions and sufficient evidence suggests that the assumptions are far closer to religious beliefs than to evidence-based programs that policymakers call for in the early years of the 21st century. Well-intentioned civic and business leaders have done what so many other reformers have been accused of in past decades: They have experimented on teachers and students for the past quarter-century without showing much evidence of success.

So I return to where I began. Fear of foreign competition and fiercely held beliefs that education harnessed to upgrading worker skills will bolster the nation's global market position prompted sustained political involvement by a variety of leaders twice in the past century. Although there have been limits to what business-led alliances could achieve, particularly in shaping what occurs in classrooms, these market-driven coalitions have produced many changes in public schooling. Above all, in the last quarter-century they have hammered into the public mind one ideological version of "good" schools and "good" teaching for all students even though evidence supporting this one-best-model is scant.

The issue is *not* whether schools should prepare students for productive work. They should. The issue is that the single-minded pursuit of preparing all students for college and high-paying jobs has narrowed the far broader and historic mission of civic engagement. The feverish quest for workplace preparation has pushed serious questions off current political agendas for school reform. Do schools geared to preparing skilled workers also build literate, independent-thinking, morally sensitive adults who carry out their civic duties in a democracy? When the economy hiccups, unemployment increases, and graduates have little money to secure higher education or find jobs matched to their skills, will public schools, now an arm of the economy, get blamed—as they have in the past—for the mismatch? And finally, in reducing the notion of a "good" age-graded school and "good" teaching to a uniform curriculum and one brand of instruction, where are the many versions of "good" schools and teaching that have prevailed in public schools in the past century and that are the current hallmark of private schools and higher education?

These basic questions, unasked by business-inspired reform coalitions over the past century, go unaddressed today. No democracy that provides tax-supported education and wants its graduates to be literate, independent, civic-minded, socially responsible adults who appreciate productive labor can afford to neglect these questions. They need to be asked now and publicly by business and civic leaders, parents, educators, students, and taxpayers. I will ask these questions and offer answers in my next two lectures.

2

Why Is It So Hard to Get More "Good" Schools?

*[A good education] teaches you how to ask a question...
it is knowing what you don't know.*

*Ideally, one should know who Shakespeare was and why Shakespeare was impor-
tant to us.... At the same time, one should know who Toni Morrison is
and why her voice and take on America is important to us."*

*An educated high school grad must read, compute, persevere, organize, and prob-
lem-solve well enough not just to attend college, but to graduate from college.*

[A good education should instill] a love of lifelong learning.
—New York City educators responding to a journalist's question about what
makes a good education, 2001[1]

In my first lecture, I claimed that twice in the last century business-led
reform coalitions have had enormous influence on shaping school curriculum, governance, and management but much less influence on changing prevailing teaching practices. Although the historic job of tax-supported public
schools has been to build literate, civic-minded, and socially responsible
adults, by the year 2000, American public schools had become an arm of the
economy. Moreover, a contemporary coalition of business and union leaders, public officials, and educators had created an educational orthodoxy of
what constitutes a "good" age-graded school and "good" teaching, one in
which most parents and taxpayers fully agreed.

In this lecture, I argue that reducing the notion of a "good" school and "good" teaching to an age-graded school with a uniform curriculum, one brand of instruction, and one kind of testing—the current official ideology—undermines public education in a democracy. It does so because the present orthodoxy ignores the many different kinds of "good" schools and teaching in the past century that have responded to the competing purposes of tax-supported public schools and the diversity of students in their motivation, backgrounds, and academic talents.

So let me take you on a brief tour of the competing beliefs (and values) that have marked the history of public schools over exactly what is a "good" school. Previous contentiousness reveals clearly the legitimacy of other versions of "good" schools. That history may puncture the official orthodoxy of a one-best-school and answer the question I ask this evening: Why is it so hard to get more "good" schools?

In the last lecture I documented the conflicts between business-minded progressive reformers in the late 19th century who wanted both vocational education in schools and student-centered teaching practices. They fought traditionalists who then guarded academic subjects and teacher-centered instruction. Continuing throughout the 20th century there has been conflict among educators, public officials, researchers, and parents over whether traditional or progressive ways of teaching reading, math, and other subjects are best. Struggles over teaching phonics or "whole language" have had parallels in math over how much emphasis should be given to learning multiplication tables, acquiring a deeper understanding of math concepts, and the skills of real-life problem solving.[2]

This unrelenting century-long struggle between traditionalists and progressives for the one best way of teaching reading and math is linked to the enduring search, past and present, for the "good" school. Are schools with high test scores that send most of their students to college "good"? Are schools that seek to develop the "whole child" "good"? Are schools where students study and work in their neighborhoods and larger community "good"? Are schools where children and adults practice democracy in and out of their classrooms on a daily basis "good"?

These questions reveal two familiar realities that too often are neglected. First, the multiple versions of "good" schools reflect the competing and historic purposes of public schools and challenge the arrogant certainty that business leaders, U.S. presidents, state governors, school boards, and pollsters express today when they describe *the* "good" school. Second, students thrive in very different types of schools. Even if you share the current view of what constitutes a "good" school, please join me—at least for the duration of this lecture—in departing from the contemporary blueprint to consider other versions, past and present, of "good" schools.

I offer vignettes of four actual schools that I unimaginatively call A, B, C, and D. These schools and their students clearly differ from one another. I claim that all four are "good."

Schools A and B are located in a middle-class California community in which parents choose the schools children attend. Both schools also have staffs that chose to work there. And both schools have been in existence for 25 years. Listen carefully.[3]

SCHOOL A

- This is a quiet, orderly school where the teacher's authority is openly honored by both students and parents.
- Drill and practice are parts of each teacher's daily lesson.
- Teachers say: "We liked the way we were taught so we teach the same way; we expect kids to adapt to our standards."
- From a first-grade classroom: Children learn how to spell six new words a day.
- From a fourth-grade classroom: Children draw up charts on early explorers.
- Report cards with letter grades are sent home every 9 weeks. Once a week, teachers send home mini-report cards.
- Parent: "If my kid can truly do something better, I want her to be asked to do it over again until it's done right. That's what they do here."
- Principal of school: "Our kids are happiest when taking a test. The more challenged they are, the better they perform. The harder they work, the better they feel about themselves."
- Parent: "Creativity can't occur until the building blocks are in place. If you are good at sports, you scrimmage. If you're good at music, you practice the scales."

SCHOOL B

- This school prizes freedom for students and teachers to pursue their interests.

- Most classrooms are multiage (6- to 9-year-olds and 7- to 11-year-olds).
- Students call most of the teachers by their first names.
- Every teacher encourages student-initiated projects.
- Students begin each day by making up their schedule of what they will do.
- Teacher: "We trust children to make the right choices."
- Principal: "We don't compare John with Sara; we compare John with John."
- Students take only those standardized tests required by the state.
- In this school, there are no spelling bees, no accelerated reading program, no letter or numerical grades. Instead, there is a five-page, year-end narrative in which a teacher describes the personal growth of each student.
- Teacher: "Learning demands no one skill. It's auditory, social, verbal, visual, and kinetic. So it's our responsibility to respond to the needs of children who have different ways of understanding the world."

On most points, then, Schools A and B differed in what parents, teachers, and students valued about knowledge, school organization, teaching, learning, and freedom. Yet each school enjoyed enthusiastic endorsement from its community.

The evidence for support is both clear and strong:

- Annual surveys of parent and student opinion have registered praise for each school.
- Each school has had a waiting list of parents who wish to enroll their sons and daughters.
- Teacher turnover at each school has been virtually nil.

Moreover, by most student-outcome measures, both schools have compiled enviable records. In academic achievement, measured by standardized tests, School A was in the top 10% of schools in the entire state. School B was in the upper half of the state's schools.

Turn now to School C.

SCHOOL C

Again, here is a verbal collage of images but they will be taken from a composite of actual schools, past and present, which have shared these common features. This high school of about one thousand students is in a working-class neighborhood of a large city. The high school, housed in a decaying building, had experienced declining academic achievement and poor attendance. High teacher turnover each year created vacancies that were filled with inexperienced teachers. The parent-teacher association had dissolved.

A new principal came to the school 5 years ago and brought with her a cadre of experienced teachers from a school where they had created a community-based school program. Here are some activities and quotations drawn from the school over the past 5 years.

- A 12th-grade government class prepared a map of the eight blocks that surround the high school with symbols for stores, bars, police station, park, and abandoned homes and cars. They posted the map in the main hallway and had a sign-up list for student volunteers to help city workers clear abandoned cars and trash from empty lots.
- A 10th-grade science class worked with a retired biologist to test water in the nearby park creek for pollutants.
- A teacher for each grade was released for one period a day to make home visits.
- A half-dozen volunteers provided childcare in school for parents at a school site council meeting.
- Ninth- and 10th-grade classes spent a half-day tutoring first-graders at nearby elementary schools.
- Principal: "My aim [is] to bring the community into the school, so that our youngsters might better grow into . . . participating citizens."
- Parent: "We asked the principal to do something about a rash of traffic accidents near the school. She got students, parents, store owners, and police officials to pitch in and clear three empty lots for the children to use as playgrounds and re-route traffic. I can't say enough about our principal."[4]

The evidence for support of School C, like Schools A and B, has been clear and strong:

- Recent surveys of parent opinion praised the community work of the school, and for the first time gave high marks to the academic program.
- Student attendance has increased by a third in the last 3 years.
- Teacher turnover at school has dropped by half.

- For the first time, over 50 neighborhood stores contributed to the scholarship fund.
- The parent-teacher group that dissolved a decade ago has been resurrected, growing from a membership of 50 the first year to 500 in the 5th year. Moreover, as measured by state standardized tests, School C has substantially improved scores.

Finally, there is School D.

SCHOOL D

Located in a large midwestern city, this K–5 school has an enrollment of almost 400 students (85% Latino and African-American) with almost 90% of the students coming from poor families. A small group of parents and teachers founded the elementary school in 1988. It has a multicultural curriculum and aims for all students to speak both Spanish and English. A steering committee of teachers and parents governs the school.

Some snippets suggest core features of School D:

- The school council of teachers, parents, a community representative, and the principal sets overall curricular, instructional, and managerial policies for the school. For example, the school council redirected funds to hire two additional teaching specialists; chose the multicultural themes that guide the program during the year; and organized the school into teaching teams of 50 to 60 students with multi-age classrooms.
- From the classroom: A resource teacher distributes a puzzle to his class: Two fathers and two sons go fishing. Each catches one fish. Everyone was successful, even though only three fish were caught. How, the teacher asks, could this have happened? Eight groups of students assign roles for each member and begin brainstorming solutions to the puzzle.
- A 4th-grade teacher was having trouble with her students' behavior when they went to a nearby river for science field trips. The behavior changed dramatically when she and the first-grade teacher planned a joint trip and the older students outdid themselves to make sure that the 6-year-olds didn't go too close to the water.
- A teacher meets with her class and, speaking Spanish, they jointly create the rules that will guide the class for the next 2-

week project.

• A teacher created a student peer-mediation program that trained children to work with one another to reduce conflicts on the playground and in school.

Parent and teacher support for School D has been constant since its founding. There is a waiting list of parents who want to send their children to the school. That standardized test scores have improved has further solidified support for the school.[5]

From these mini-verbal portraits you probably have formed an impression of each school. I suspect you even have a preference for one or more of these schools for your children, nieces, nephews, or grandchildren.[6]

For many observers, School A could be called "traditional" or "conservative" with pride by supporters and scorn by opponents of this type of schooling. School B could be called progressive or nontraditional, School C might be called community-based, and School D could be labeled as both progressive and democratic—also with pride or scorn, depending on people's preferences.

Can all of these schools be "good"? They differ dramatically from one another in size, organization, socioeconomic status, and age of student. They differ in how teachers organize their classrooms, view learning, teach the curriculum, and connect to their community. But for me, the answer is a clear, unambiguous yes.

Yet my straightforward answer that all of these schools are "good" ignores two important points. First, what made these schools "good," and, second, why has there been so much conflict, so much intolerance, in this century among policymakers, academics, parents, and taxpayers over which kind of schooling—progressive, community-based, democratic, or traditional—is best for children?

WHAT MADE THESE SCHOOLS "GOOD"?

Ideologues would probably claim that their respective beliefs about children, learning, and teaching made the difference. Let me suggest other reasons that might explain why these schools were prized by students, parents, and teachers.

For over 25 years, Schools A and B, located in middle-class communities, had committed principals and teachers—who also chose to be at each school—working closely with parents to make each what it is today. School C, on the other hand, had a new but experienced principal and teachers committed to a philosophy of making the high school an integral part of a blue-collar neighborhood regarding what was studied and how academic subjects were taught. They worked together to improve the school for 5 years. The school reached out to fill unmet community needs. In doing so, the staff used the neighborhood to teach students that where they lived was valued and needed improvement, not contempt. School D, like Schools A and B, enjoyed the unswerving support of activist parents, teachers, and leading community figures. The principal, parents, and teachers chose to be at the school.

These may well be the contextual, political, and leadership factors that made the four schools "good," rather than whether each was ideologically labeled traditional, progressive, community-based, or democratic. The century-long war of words among true believers replays familiar, if tired, arguments filled with charges and counter-charges that School A, B, C, or D is better than the others. Nor can science be dragged in to clear away the contentiousness. Educational researchers, time and again, have failed to prove that one pattern of schooling is superior to another in student learning. There is simply no scientific evidence that conclusively demonstrates that any of these schools are better forms of education for *all* students than the others.[7]

It is no surprise, then, that for this entire century there have been school wars fought among educators, public officials, researchers, and parents over which form of schooling is best for children. A quick trip through this century will establish how muscle-bound and cyclical this ideological struggle has been.[8]

In the early 20th century, varied versions of progressive schooling, drawing from the work of John Dewey and many other school reformers, swept across the country, changing curricula, partially modifying instruction, and expanding the social role of the school to take on duties that families had once discharged. Progressive reformers scorned the traditional schooling of the day with its bolted-down desks, regimented instruction, blind obedience to authority, organizational inefficiencies, and divorce from the world outside the classroom door. They wanted schools to have multi-age groups rather than tightly controlled age-graded classes. They wanted to focus on the personal and social development of students. They wanted schools to be part of the community rather than separated from it. They wanted schools to offer many curricular choices to match the diversity of students as they became citizens and entered the workplace. And they wanted schools to be both democratic and efficient in their practices and governance. By the 1930s, much of what they sought, in some places more than others and in some form or another, had been achieved.[9]

With the end of World War II and the onset of the Cold War, progressive and democratic educational ideas declined in popularity, giving way to new programs triggered by fears of the Soviet Union. U.S. leaders drafted public

All are good because they are achieving what they are determined to be the population

* when the philosophies are compatible, it is easy for schools to "be good" succeed.

schools to fight the Cold War by preparing more students in math and science to become engineers and scientists who could defend the United States against a powerful enemy. Raising academic standards and creating new programs for the intellectually gifted became benchmarks for the post-Sputnik years.[10]

Part of the Cold War ideological fight was Soviet finger-pointing at the United States's malign treatment of racial minorities. The U.S. pursuit of allies among African and Asian countries often became unhinged when lynchings in the American South and segregated schools made headlines in the world's press. Spurred by NAACP-inspired litigation, events in World War II, and Cold War rivalries, the U.S. Supreme Court declared segregated schools unconstitutional in 1954. A subsequent civil rights movement in the 1960s shifted school policy debates from programs for the gifted and rigorous math and science courses toward federal and state interventions to end segregated schools, correct social inequities, and re-focus attention on the personal and social development of students. Progressive programs such as Head Start, the Job Corps, Career Education, and "open classrooms" became high-profile, federally funded innovations.[11]

By the early 1970s, however, with the Vietnam War still dividing the country and school budgets getting cut, enthusiasm for progressive programs evaporated. Since then, a version of traditional schooling focusing on high academic standards, stronger school discipline, a standardized curriculum, and testing has become the official orthodoxy. Yet even in the late 1980s and early 1990s, forms of progressive thinking had revived among practitioners and academics around student-centered teaching, performance-based assessment, and project-based curriculum. Also, efforts to restructure schools and create new charter schools where teachers and parents independently or together run schools have generated renewed interest in democratic governance and progressive classroom practices.[12]

WHY HAS THERE BEEN A CYCLICAL STRUGGLE OF IDEAS?

I suggest two reasons for this cyclical struggle: a deeply rooted value conflict over child-rearing beliefs that has been grafted onto age-graded schooling, and a decentralized system of American education where public officials, responding to different constituencies, have prodded schools to get in step with larger social, economic, and political changes.

The first reason involves the moral politics of raising and schooling children. In the early 19th century, taxpayers, parents, and public officials saw tax-supported schools as places to extend the reach of the family's influence on children. Protestant Christianity steeped in biblical views of parental authority saw children as innately depraved and in need of guidance. Disobedience was a sin. Thus, raising children to respect authority, be self-disciplined, and know clearly right from wrong was essential in the family and expected in the one-room schoolhouses, and, later, in the age-graded schools. In school, children would become literate, God-fearing, morally upstanding, and equipped with civic virtues. This model of raising and schooling children was viewed as natural and, of course, "good."[13]

In the middle of the 19th century, another view emerged, challenging the religious-based popular model of child rearing. The onslaught of industrialization, rapid urban growth, an emerging middle class, and massive immigration spurred reformers to advocate another, more "progressive," view of how best to raise children. In this view, confined initially to manuals for middle-class parents, readers were urged to cultivate the innate goodness of children rather than dwell on their potential sinfulness. Parental love and example, not punishment, would produce respect for authority, self-discipline, and moral rigor in children.

Post–Civil War urban reformers, who saw immigrant parents working long hours and living in urban slums, thought that traditional schools were inadequate to cope with newcomers. They urged schools to expand their usual duties and take on the nurturing roles that families had once discharged. Schools should offer medical care, meals, and explicit lessons on moral character, including respect for civil authority and productive labor. Teachers were expected to develop children's intellectual, emotional, and social capacities to produce mature, community-engaged adults. These notions about an expanded social role of public schools converged with the newly emerging science of psychology and a growing urban middle class to create a rival ideology of what a "good" child, family, and school were.[14]

By World War I, then, these competing progressive and traditional beliefs already constituted different faiths in the best way of raising children. These conflicting ideologies had become embedded in educators' language and school programs, creating contrasting patterns of schooling children and a battleground over deciding what "good" schools were. This century-long seesaw struggle of beliefs over what is the best form of raising children and its application to schooling is, then, a much deeper religious conflict writ large over what role schools should play in society.

To some in the audience, my labeling the conflict "religious" may be carelessly slipping into hyperbole. I need to explain that I use the word to capture the contentious moral beliefs embedded in rival churches. What is (and has been) at stake for advocates of either progressive or traditional ways of raising children to obey authority, become self-disciplined, and act morally is literally a "best" way of schooling all children. Without scientific evidence to establish which way is better, groups from the political right and left have turned their moral convictions in how best to rear and school children into evangelical gospel. So these tensions have come to resemble century-old struggles among contending religions in Europe, the Middle East, Asia, and this country.[15]

Consider the matter of discipline. Since 1969, public opinion polls on education have asked Americans to identify the single most pressing issue they see in schools. Every year parents and nonparents named school discipline as one of the top three problems that schools needed to address. For traditionalists, cracking down on students who disobeyed school rules was the best way of teaching respect for authority. Some even sought a return of spanking. Others wanted to expel unruly students and tighten school security measures, including the presence of police.[16]

For progressives, a breakdown in school order was a community problem—growing violence in a media-saturated society—that public officials had ignored. Blaming schools for a larger social problem was scapegoating a vulnerable institution, they argued. Moreover, progressives felt strongly that resorting to corporal punishment or imposing stiff penalties for breaking rules diverted attention from deeper social problems while creating a police-state climate within schools. Progressives endorsed punishing unruly students for acts that hurt peers and the school, but they also sought nonpunitive ways of helping children become self-disciplined and respectful of others' rights.

For the past 30 years, there have been few public resolutions of these "religious" or sharp ideological differences among progressives and traditionalists over the single best way to deal with school discipline. These ideological struggles over discipline—and I could just as easily have added debates over homework, standardized achievement test scores, phonics, tracking students, or even school uniforms—illustrate the deeper and more pervasive moral imperative shaping how families raise their children. A strong link, then, exists between the moral and the political, between the family and the school, between child-rearing practices and schooling the child.

Thus, contested ideas over rearing children have shaped national and local debates between traditionalists and progressives over what kind of schooling all children should receive. In a democracy, where voters can express their opinions about officials and taxes at the ballot box and where authority to govern schools is widely dispersed—there are, after all, nearly 15,000 districts in 50 states to govern nearly 50 million children in 90,000 public schools—the issue of "good" schools has often become politically contested by rival moral faiths seeking their versions of "goodness."

And this highly decentralized system of public schooling is the second reason for these long-running ideological wars: Democratic politics demand that school boards and superintendents respond to those constituencies pressing for changes. At the turn of the last century, temperance reformers secured from school boards mandatory courses on alcohol, tobacco, and drug abuse. Before World War I, elite groups' nervousness over immigrants' different languages and customs overwhelming the dominant culture led to school boards adopting Americanization programs. After World War II, activists deeply committed to social justice mobilized support for the Civil Rights Act of 1964 and the Education for All Handicapped Children Act of 1975. And, more recently, business-led coalitions have convinced governors and legislators to mandate higher academic standards, test students often, and buy computers.[17]

Why have state and local school boards and superintendents been so responsive to constituents? The answer is self-evident: To survive, public schools must have the political and financial support of voters and taxpayers. Surely, some very large school district boards and administrators, at different times, have been able to insulate themselves from voter disaffection—but not for long. Recall that in the previous lecture, I pointed out how in the late 19th century market-driven reformers steered public schools toward a progressive version of "good" schools through vocational education and in the past quarter century, business-minded reformers have urged on all students a traditional academic schooling. There is a truth about democratic politics buried in the cliché: When the nation has a cold, public schools sneeze.

CONCLUSIONS

These two reasons (differences in values over how best to raise children and the schools' responsiveness to their constituencies in a dispersed system of school governance) help explain the periodic conflicts between progressive and traditional beliefs about schooling over the past century. But offering reasons for why a problem exists is not the same as solving it.

And that is why I offered descriptions of four schools. They represent for me a way out of this impasse over which kind of schooling, which kind of "religion," is viewed as better than the other. I argue that all four schools are "good." One is clearly traditional in its concentration on passing on to children the best knowledge, skills, and values in society. One is avowedly progressive in its focus on multi-age groupings and the personal and social development of individuals. And another is a mix of traditional academics and progressive ideas in making the community a part of the school's curriculum. The fourth is explicitly multicultural, progressive, and democratic in governance and classroom practices. Each asserts that it serves different values. Each teaches its own brand of knowledge and skills. Each puts into practice what it seeks to achieve. Each uses emotionally loaded words to describe what it does. Each has thrived in urban slums, working-class neighborhoods, and suburban ghettos.

Yet—and this is the basic point that I wish to stress—these goals, practices, and vocabulary, different as they appear, strongly worded as they are for public consumption, still derive from a common framework of what these apparently opposing groups of reformers and parents want their public schools to achieve. Opinion polls, referenda on school issues, and frequent reference to the historical legacy of common schools reveal that both progressives and traditionalists want students to put into practice the knowledge they gain, display in their behavior the moral attitudes they learned, and use skills acquired in school. Both progressives and traditionalists respond to differences in students' interests, motivation, talents, and backgrounds. Both want their children to become literate, self-disciplined, self-reliant adults engaged in productive work, and committed to sustaining democratic practices in their communities and the nation.[18]

But to anyone who has sampled media reports on public schools recently or heard top policymakers discuss schooling, little time or space is devoted to these shared common purposes binding together those who have historically battled over discipline and phonics. There is much that progressives and traditionalists share. Instead, what we see in the media are constant references to ongoing culture wars. And that is because for the last quarter-century, opinion leaders have argued that the middle class is torn up over an internal culture war between conservative and liberal values on abortion, homosexuality, and multiculturalism. When middle-class folks, white and black, immigrant and native, speak their minds, however, the commonalities that bind together progressives and traditionalists emerge clearly.[19]

What is far more powerful than media-driven culture wars, however, is the growing consensus among top policymakers and business elites that ties the fortunes of the United States in the global economy to how well public schools are preparing the next generation of workers. The gold standard for the adequacy of that preparation has become published test scores.

Recall that in my description of the four schools, I too used test scores and other performance measures. I implied that all of these schools were improving or had done well on these outcomes. Therefore, they were "good."

I did so because the prevailing political realities require attention to test scores since they have become the only legitimate standard for judging effectiveness and ultimately the "goodness" of a school. But attention to raising test scores is not the same as restricting the school's agenda to those tests. And it is that wiggle room between selective attention to tests and a sole focus on scoring better that Schools B, C, and D have maneuvered in order to retain their "goodness."

None of these schools could escape standardized tests. School A welcomed the competition and scorekeeping. Schools B, C, and D paid attention to scores for political reasons connected to their survival but carped at the time they had to spend on preparing students for these tests while still steering a course toward goals that were far less easy to measure.

And, of course, it is this current political orthodoxy that contains the answer to my question: Why is it so hard to get more "good" schools in American education? So let me end by summing up my answer.

First, notions of "goodness" in schools have varied for centuries. These diverse values reflect a deep reluctance among Americans to define a "good" society, a "good" person, and how best to worship God. What has happened in the past century, however, is that these varied notions of "goodness," particularly about rearing children, have been grafted onto schools, become politicized, and gotten mired in the century-long debate between traditionalists and progressives to prove that one version of "good" teaching and a "good" school is best.[20]

Second, aggressive political coalitions pressing for their value-driven agendas and school officials' responsiveness to such lobbying have produced changes in school goals, curriculum, management, and governance while retaining the familiar age-graded school organization. In the last quarter century, business-led coalitions have triumphed extraordinarily in engineering an armor-plated accountability machine that imposes serious consequences on mediocre students and schools while spreading an official orthodoxy of what constitutes a "good" school for the 21st century. The inability of policymakers or researchers to demonstrate conclusively which policies or practices are scientifically superior has kept the ideological warfare alive.

And in that battle, contemporary school reformers have triumphed in securing more School As rather than versions B, C, and D. In linking better schools to a better economy, market-minded reformers have fastened onto schools the heavy load of standardized test scores as the sole determinant of goodness, thus weakening the hold that other versions of "good" schools have had for decades. A striking example of this feverish quest for sameness occurred in 2001. The Scarsdale (New York) public schools boycotted the new Regents tests. This is a district where students who take the Scholastic Assessment Test (SAT) score, on average, 1286, and where 90% of eighth graders pass the state tests at double the rate for schools in the rest of the state. State Commissioner of Education Richard Mills, who supported portfolios, performance-based writing, and other progressive teaching practices when he served as Vermont's top school officer, responded to Scarsdale's test boycott by saying: "I can't ignore what they did. We're looking for uniformity."[21]

In taking for granted the age-graded school as the vehicle for learning and test scores as precious coin of the realm that must be heeded, triumphant reformers have sought uniformity and forgotten that there are more ways than one to define "goodness" in schools. They have dismissed the realities of how dominant views of race, social class, and intelligence influence school organization, curriculum, and instruction in dealing with differences among students in their talents, interests, and backgrounds as "racist nonsense." They have failed to acknowledge openly the hybrids of "good" schools in the past and now. School A, for example, traditional as it is, still has classrooms where students and teacher jointly make rules to govern their time together. School C is community-oriented yet has a traditional age-graded school organization and governance. Finally, they have ignored the obvious fact that in the United States private schools and higher education—both public and private—are built on the principle that different schools are "good" for different students.[22]

We need to recover from the present and the past the simple fact that for over 150 years many versions of "good" schools existed in public and private education and publish that fact in 72-point boldface type. We also need to expand the historical and contemporary variety of goodness in schools for no other reason than that in this democracy, there is no one best way to think, no one best way to worship one's God, no one best way to live a life, and no one best way to school a child. The quest for a one-best system is a fool's errand when it comes to choosing one's religious faith, one's philosophy of life, or one's school. What the most recent business-inspired reform coalition has demanded from schools (and most, but not all, parents have endorsed) is a traditional blueprint of a "good" school, one that has been part of a long, enduring historic struggle over rival ways of educating the young.

And, ultimately, that is why "good" schools are hard to get. It is not because of an absence of ideas or expertise or a lack of will. Then and now, parents, rich and poor, white and black, urban and rural, working closely with educators, have created "good" schools. "Good" schools are hard to get because of an evangelical, almost tyrannical, faith in establishing *one* version of what is a "good" school. They are hard to get because few corporate leaders, public officials, and practitioners have examined carefully, deliberately, and openly the different purposes public schools serve and the different conceptions of "goodness" that flow from those purposes. Nor have reformers considered how each view of a "good" school is connected to ideas of child-rearing and democratic responsiveness. They are hard to get because color- and class-blind reformers, with the best of intentions, either fail to see or ignore how race and social-class stratification persist outside schools and are amplified in a one-best system for all children.

Until present-day reformers openly recognize that parents, principals, and teachers have already made many kinds of "good" schools, and until they develop explicit criteria that go beyond the single-minded training of students for the workplace to include the nourishing of civic virtue, the current official orthodoxy will prevail. The tyranny of a one-best-school model that largely seeks to prepare individual students for an information-based workplace ultimately weakens public schooling in a democracy because it ignores the fundamental purpose of public schooling as revitalizing democratic practices and building a strong sense of a common good in each generation while ensuring that the young are prepared for productive labor.

It is these criteria for a "good" school and the recovery of both democratic purposes and practices in and out of school that I turn to in my final lecture.

3

How Do We Get More "Good" Schools?

The chief end [of public schools] is to make GOOD CITIZENS. Not to make pre-cocious scholars ... not to impart the secret of acquiring wealth ... not to qualify for professional success ... but simply to make good citizens.
—Illinois Superintendent of Public Instruction, 1862 (emphasis in original)[1]

Education ... is the very foundation of good citizenship.
—Brown v. Board of Education, 1954[2]

The [U.S.] Supreme Court has long recognized that public education is meant to assist students to become "self-reliant and self-sufficient participants in society."—
Campaign for Fiscal Equity et al. v. The State of New York et al., 2001[3]

In the first two lectures, I argued that market-inspired reformers in the past century twice succeeded in tying public schools to the U.S. economy. Moreover, in the past quarter-century, business-minded reformers forged, with parental endorsement, a value consensus that a "good" school has a uniform curriculum, teacher-centered instruction, and tests aimed at preparing all students for college and jobs in an information-based workplace. Capping this agreement on a "good" school is the "bottom line" for students, teachers, and principals: improved test scores. As important as it is to have students appreciate productive labor and perform well on tests that accurately meas-ure what they have learned, I left no doubt in the last lecture that this official orthodoxy is bad for American public education since these beliefs subordi-nate civic purposes to workplace preparation and individual social mobility

39

while ignoring the historic diversity of "good" schools.

I offered four examples of "good" schools: traditional, progressive, community-based, and democratic. I claimed that all four were "good" because, even though their practices differed, students became literate, parents endorsed the schools, and each in its own way worked to create adults who sought both the common good and personal success. I ended that lecture by chiding market-inspired reformers for their quasi-religious fervor in creating a one-best-kind of school and, in doing so, overwhelming the historic and core purpose for public schooling in a democracy: building literate, civic-minded, morally responsible citizens who appreciate useful work.

Many of those who heard the last lecture may have left feeling puzzled over where I would go in this final one. Can I offer a way out of this ideological tyranny that I claim currently exists? As a historian of education and a practitioner, I can do no less than try. The title of this final lecture is "How Do We Get More 'Good' Schools?" and the opening quotations about the centrality of citizenship to public schooling suggest the direction I will travel this evening.

Now wouldn't it be easy for both of us if I would pause, clear my throat to effect a baritone register, and shift character from being a scholar to becoming an educational Zeus speaking in a thundering voice while hurling lightning-bolt prescriptions for creating "good" schools? I would list in catchy phrasings the 5 or 10 actions that earnest educators and parents must do to get "good" schools. The practitioner part of me yearns for that certitude. But the historian part of me asks: How can I give out formulas when I have been a severe critic of others who marketed reform recipes? And it is to that scholarly part of me that I finally listen. Yet be warned: Although historians seldom give prescriptions, they do give headaches. So prepare yourself for a migraine.

To answer the question on how to get more "good" schools and in light of the four examples I gave in the last lecture, my response requires answering two prior questions: "Good" for what and "good" for whom? These questions probe at the past and present purposes of public schooling in a democracy—the "good for what?" question—and the remarkable diversity in students who attend public schools—the "good for whom?" question.

"GOOD" FOR WHAT?

I turn first to the historic multiple and conflicting purposes of American schools. Please note that defining the purposes of public education in relation to what "good" schools are is neither trivial nor an academic exercise. Determining what constitutes a "good" school has been closely tied to federal and state court decisions in California, Texas, New Jersey, Kentucky, and, most recently, New York when State Supreme Court Justice Leland DeGrasse declared that a constitutionally "sound basic education" was lacking for the children of New York City. These decisions had (and have) major consequences for funding preschool education, getting qualified and adequately paid teachers, reorganizing age-graded schools, buying sufficient books and computers, and many other outcomes reaching into thousands of classrooms. So purposes matter.[4]

Yet there have been (and are) many purposes for public schools. Building literate and moral citizens committed to democratic equality, preparing skilled workers for a changing economy, and helping individuals achieve personal success have been explicit purposes for historically forcing taxpayers to open their wallets to pay for public schools. These purposes combine a search for the collective good with parents' deeply personal (and private) wish for their sons and daughters to move up the social-class escalator. [5]

Complicating the choice among important purposes are the inevitable economic, social, political, and demographic changes that unpredictably sweep across the American landscape. So often these societal changes produce messy problems that spur urgent calls for schools to solve them. Recall from the late 19th century business leaders' fears of foreign competition for American products leading to successfully putting industrial education into American schools or citizen activists' fears that alcohol and tobacco abuse needed remedies. Because available school funds have seldom matched the magnitude of problems laid at the schoolhouse's door, reformers have often skirmished over which of the change-driven social and economic problems facing schools should be addressed and which of these multiple purposes should be primary and which secondary. As a result, elected officials often negotiated tangled compromises among these purposes.[6]

A clear example of such a compromise is one of the eight national goals that the past two U.S. presidents and George W. Bush have approved for all public schools.

> By the year 2000, all students will leave grades 4, 8, and 12 having demonstrated competency over challenging subject matter including English, mathematics, science, foreign languages, civics and government, economics, arts, history, and geography, and every school in America will ensure that all students learn to use their minds well, so they may be prepared for responsible citizenship, further learning, and productive employment in our Nation's modern economy. (Goal 3: Student Achievement and Citizenship, 1995)[7]

Note the logic of the goal. Knowledge of and achievement in academic subjects, as measured by standardized test scores, lead to civic virtue, college, and jobs. This theory of action is popular and unquestioned. As my first lecture pointed out, a major problem with the theory is that there is very little evidence to support it. Also popular and unquestioned is the assumption in this national goal that it applies to all students, thus easily answering the question: "good" for whom?

"GOOD" FOR WHOM?

For the past two decades, corporate leaders, public officials, and educators who have steered the standards-based, test-driven accountability movement have adopted the popular slogan: "All children can learn." Regardless of ethnicity, race, social class, or disability, all students—they say—can acquire the skills, gain the knowledge, meet the standards, do well on the tests, and go to college. They claim that to expect less from poor and minority children is bigotry. Having claimed the moral high ground of deep concern for the poor, children of color, and those with disabilities, few have openly challenged this slogan.

Consider, however, all those 4- and 5-year olds, including low-income minority children, who enter age-graded schools for the first time. Each child, regardless of background, health, and previous experiences, certainly has the capacity and desire to learn. But each is expected to take the same amount of time to learn a chunk of the pre-set curriculum and then demonstrate that learning in order to move to the next grade and the next and the next until graduation. The age-graded school and its inexorable time schedule sandpaper off the differences among children to slide them into bins marked "normal." But many don't easily fit.

So it should come as no surprise that every generation of children moving through these age-graded schools has contained small to large percentages of students who cannot keep pace. These laggards either end up repeating the grade or, because they have been held back before and are older than classmates, are moved to the next grade—a practice called "social promotion" and detested by many standards-driven reformers.[8]

In the past century, school staffs have labeled students who performed poorly in the age-graded school "slow learners," "pupils of low I.Q.," "disadvantaged," or similar terms for lacking the smarts to master the age-graded curriculum in the prescribed amount of time. Instead of questioning the time-to-learn imperative buried in the age-graded school, most educators have historically blamed students and their families for academic failure.[9]

Beginning in the late 1970s, however, Effective Schools reformers reframed the problem of failing students by pointing to failing schools. "Disadvantaged" or "at-risk" students who did poorly in their academic subjects were not at fault. The fault was in teachers' and administrators' low expectations, a flabby curriculum, and a school climate hostile to learning. According to these reformers, such factors depressed student achievement. Ineffective schools, not the students, were the problem. None of these reformers, however, pointed to the age-graded school as a factor.[10]

The current standards-based movement, drawing heavily on Effective Schools rhetoric and theories, avoids blaming students directly for failing academically—remember, "all students can learn" is its celebrated motto. They too take for granted the age-graded school. And the reasons they do are clear. We live in a socially stratified society where inequities in income and position are clear to anyone watching television or driving around a city and its suburbs. The goal of social mobility that all parents seek for their children requires the awarding of selective and differential school credentials. The age-graded school is simply an institutional agent for separating those children who succeed from those who fail. The tremendous opposition to social promotion is partially anchored in this search for ways to give individual children a competitive advantage over their peers. So in the solutions that business-inspired reformers have marketed successfully, those students who can't read by the end of the third grade or later drop out still bear the full burden of failure.[11]

To be specific: The standards-based curricula and tests require low-performing students to take more college-bound courses, spend more time in remedial classes during the day and after school, and often go to summer school. If these don't help students pass the required test, they repeat the year in the same grade or the subject or, after repeated failures, drop out.

Reformers are praised for their unflinching support to the principle of giving students equal access to a demanding curriculum, regardless of whether certified teachers are in classrooms, how large the class is, how students vary in the time they need to learn, or whether students need glasses. Reformers are praised for their unblinking courage in holding students to high academic standards and denying high school diplomas to those students who don't measure up. Yet few of the staunchest advocates of standards-based reform consider creating different kinds of "good" schools to prevent failure in the typical age-graded school or providing other resources to achieve a different version of equal opportunity.[12]

Thus, the claim that all children can learn—splendid in its appeal to color- and class-blindness and its devotion to equal access—is only the beginning of a paragraph. The full paragraph should read: All children can learn *if* state legislatures provide schools with adequate funds, if all children are healthy and ready for school, if they have certified teachers earning adequate salaries, small class size, and sufficient time to learn according to their stages of intellectual and social development. We only hear from passionate reformers the opening sentence, seldom the crucial word *if* and what follows it.

At issue here are at least two definitions of equality of educational opportunity. Everyone getting the same chance to perform is the equal access version. Nondiscrimination is unassailable for those who pride themselves on seeing no color or class system in America, no deep social structures strengthening inequality that undercut an individual's will and capacity to learn and achieve. The reigning metaphor is the meritocratic race where everyone has the same chance to win the gold medal.[13]

A competing definition of equality acknowledges that concepts of race, gender, class, and ethnicity are deeply embedded in social attitudes, practices, and structures that shape what students bring to school and a school staff's response to their students' strengths and limitations. The job of the school and the community is to level the playing field. This affirmative-action version of equality gives unequal help to those children who— through no fault of their own—need assistance in schools, particularly in efforts to close the achievement gap between minority and white children.

Parents, of course, are caught in the middle of these competing definitions of equality. On the one hand, they are committed to treating their sons and daughters equally and expecting high performance from them. They also acknowledge, on the other hand, differences among their children and treat them unequally: getting a math tutor for Benjamin while sending Beth to a camp for gifted children. Both states and the federal government have embraced the two versions of equal educational opportunity. Except for Title I of the Elementary and Secondary Education Act, after-school programs, and special education—which try to level the playing field—federal and state governments have largely pursued an equal-access, color- and class-blind view of equality.

In the present standards-based, testing, and accountability orthodoxy of a "good" school, the meritocratic version of equal access in order to produce high performance commands the most attention from state and federal officials. The level-playing-field view of providing unequal treatment in order to provide equal access—except for traditional (and limited) federal and state funding of special programs—was largely abandoned a decade ago with the dumping of "opportunity-to-learn" standards. After that policy debate fizzled, few federal or state officials pressed legislatures to send more funds to under-resourced districts to provide Head Start for all eligible students, smaller class size, and higher salaries to attract certified teachers to serve in low-performing schools. [14]

Still, the importance of differential treatment for the minority poor continues to show up in New York, California, and other states where litigants have dragged this definition of equality of educational opportunity back into the courts and sparked a larger policy debate over what resources are necessary to school low-income children. Equal access is not enough; unequal treatment is essential for students whose needs differ greatly and vary in motivation, interests, aptitudes, and background. These inescapable tensions between differing versions of equal educational opportunity show up repeatedly in determining which schools are "good" and why.[15]

In answering the questions "good" for what and "good" for whom, I have laid out the importance of purposes for tax-supported public schools and the awesome diversity of students who enter and leave public schools. I connected both answers to so many school reformers' silence over, or swift dismissal of, such matters as family poverty, inadequate funding of schools, unqualified teachers, and large class size. I suggested that the sentence "All children can learn" should be made into a paragraph ending in a punch line that calls attention to under-funded schools, poverty, and a variety of "good" schools to reduce the intractable gap in test scores between minority and white students and the predictable annual failure of so many students.

Finally, I underscored the unchallenged dominance of the age-graded school and its rigid time schedule for learning as being responsible for sorting students into those who succeed and those who fail, giving some a distinct advantage in the subsequent quest for credentials, high-paying jobs, and elevated social status. The evidence of the past century makes clear that substantial numbers of students have been labeled misfits for no other reason than not keeping pace with the age-graded school clock. Largely unquestioned throughout the past century except for occasional innovations with young children, the age-graded school remains the one best way to organize and govern a "good" school—except for the four schools that I defined as "good."[16]

REDEFINING "GOOD" SCHOOLS

Two of the schools defined as "good" were age-graded, and two had combinations of multi-aged classes mixed in with the traditional structures. Obviously, having an age-graded structure is neither a requirement nor a criterion for "goodness"; it is a choice that teachers, parents, and others make. I mention the two schools (B and D) that had multi-age classes to make clear that redefining what a "good" school is includes reorganizing the traditional division of children by age and grade. Unfortunately, many reformers have overlooked the central role that school organization and its use of time has played in shaping teachers', parents', and students' ideas about teaching, learning, and knowledge. They have assumed that the age-graded school is as natural as the sun rising and setting. It is not.[17]

To begin the task of redefining a "good" school, then, I have to be clear about the criteria that I use. Note well that the word *criteria* refers to a value, a standard by which one can make a judgment. Thus, in offering these criteria, my values enter the discussion.

In describing the four schools, I have already suggested parent, student, and teacher satisfaction as a reasonable standard to use in determining a "good" school. These core constituencies often spell the difference between success and failure of schooling, and the degree to which they are satisfied gives political legitimacy and support to the institution. [18]

I would add a second criterion: To what degree has a public school achieved its own explicit goals? Opinion polls and votes on school taxes and referenda reveal that both progressives and traditionalists want their children to become literate, civic-minded, self-disciplined, and self-reliant adults engaged in worthwhile work. Both progressives and traditionalists want their public schools to inculcate in the next generation democratic values and behaviors. So, for those who worry that letting parents, teachers, and other members of the school community determine their goals might lead to strange outcomes, based on polls, referenda, and direct experience in urban and suburban districts I have few doubts about which goals most adults will choose. [19]

In addition to different constituencies' satisfaction and each school's achieving goals that it sets, there is a third and final standard to judge "goodness" that some of you may have already anticipated.

Recall that I claimed that the fundamental purpose of tax-supported schooling in the United States has been to produce literate, self-reliant, morally responsible graduates who display democratic behaviors and attitudes. When I use grand phrases like "self-reliant adults" and "democratic attitudes," listeners desperately try to stifle yawns. It seems so boring to note the strong linkage between public schools and voting, serving on juries, and joining neighbors to improve a community. Boring or not, these behaviors are the forms of civic engagement that most Americans, regardless of their views about goodness in schools, desire for themselves and their children. [20]

Within these common values that I claim both traditionalists and progressives share, exactly what do I mean by democratic attitudes and behaviors? A brief, albeit partial, list may help:

- Participation in and willingness to serve in local and national communities.
- Open-mindedness to different opinions and a willingness to listen to such opinions.
- Respect for values that differ from one's own.
- Treating individuals decently and fairly, regardless of background.

• A commitment to reason through problems and struggle toward openly arrived at compromises.

Such democratic virtues are, of course, learned in families, at work, and in the community. In schools, learning democratic attitudes and behaviors requires students to become literate, display critical-thinking skills, and further develop their intellectual powers. As one New York Supreme Court Justice put it:

> Productive citizenship means more than just being *qualified* to vote or serve as a juror, but to do so capably and knowledgeably. It connotes civic engagement. An engaged, capable voter needs the intellectual tools to evaluate complex issues, such as campaign finance reform, tax policy, and global warming, to name only a few. (Emphasis in original)[21]

Yet educating for civic engagement can mean what the jurist said and it can mean other things to parents, educators, researchers, and policymakers—all of whom are committed to what they call democracy. For some, civic engagement may mean taking personal responsibility to vote and serve on a jury. For others, it may mean serious participation in a broad range of community and government activities. For still others, civic engagement may mean literate students' collectively deliberating and participating in activities that try to actually improve neighborhood or community conditions. The varied meanings of citizenship and democracy cover such diverse in-school activities as mock elections, students and teachers making classroom rules, older children tutoring younger ones, and class projects involving neighborhood organizations. As the research of Joel Westheimer and Joseph Kahne have made clear, each of us might favor one or more of these versions of civic engagement. There is no one way to teach or practice civic engagement or democracy. Disagreement over what are the best ways of teaching, practicing civic participation, and assessing the results should not obscure that it remains a core standard for judging goodness in a school.[22]

What matters in judging whether schools are "good," then, is not whether they are progressive, community-based, or traditional but whether they are discharging their primary duty to seriously and deliberately educate students to think and act democratically inside and outside of classrooms.

But how can educators, parents, and taxpayers ever determine whether schools have achieved these important outcomes? Certainly, existing standardized tests measure aspects of literacy but hardly come close to what I suggest. The progressive, community-based, and democratic schools that I described in my last lecture have informal measures of success but lack short- and long-term assessments that would fully capture their activities and outcomes. There have been previous efforts to create multiple nontest assessments but they have faded from the memories of current educators and public officials. New measures would have to be constructed. It is a tough but not an impossible task.[23]

Here, then, are my criteria for judging whether a school is "good":

- Are parents, staff, and students satisfied with what occurs in the school?
- Is the school achieving the explicit goals that it has set for itself?
- Are democratic behaviors, values, and attitudes evident in the students?

If quantitative and qualitative data collected from a particular school including its staff, students, and parents display an overall positive picture, then I would say the school is "good."

Now, let me ask some hard questions about what I am proposing. Am I being utopian in reaffirming school and district autonomy when the trend over the past quarter-century is clearly toward state and federal centralization and uniformity? Perhaps. In our federal system of governance there have been constant tensions for over two centuries in determining the proper locus of authority for particular decisions. Constitutionally and historically, education has been a state and local concern. Will education become another state responsibility that has become nationalized like interstate highways? It appears to be moving in that direction. But if it were to occur, the loss of local participation in school decision-making would be unfortunate. Local autonomy is critical in making choices about what goals to pursue, how to organize schools, and what and how to teach, particularly so in the absence of scientific evidence to prove that one form of schooling is superior to another. Localities differ dramatically and local decision-making offers ways for school boards to tailor their schools to fit particular contexts.

Yes, some choices made by districts and schools may be awful. That happens in democracies. And within a multilevel governance arrangement where federal authorities check state and local actions there are ways, slow as they may be, to curb harmful excesses. Southern segregated schools in the 1950s, for example, began to change sluggishly in the wake of the *Brown* decision, the civil rights movement, and federal intervention, but change they did. No one I know has ever promoted democracy for its efficiency.

Am I utopian in urging that we recover the historic centrality of civic virtues at a time when national and state policymakers have made schools an arm of the economy? I don't think so. When the economy sours and graduates can't find jobs or take low-paying ones, or they find college too expensive, it is not market-driven reforms that get blamed but schools themselves.

Yet school board members neither design economic policies, create jobs, nor hand out unemployment benefits. National and state leaders do.[24]

And that is the trap set when business-inspired reformers steer schools toward serving the economy. If there are fewer high-paying jobs available or graduates take jobs below what their credentials promised, then the fault is the school's and the individual's, not federal fiscal and monetary policies, corporate decisions to avoid paying taxes, or overinvest in technologies, or simply mismanagement. Blaming school boards, superintendents, principals, teachers, and individual students for failing takes the spotlight off corporate behavior, federal economic policies, and the deeper societal structures that maintain social inequalities.

No trap, however, awaits those corporate leaders, public officials, parents, and educators who restore civic engagement to the keystone purpose it once held. Recovering civic mindedness as a central purpose breaks the chain tying schools to a boom-and-bust economic cycle and forges new links between literacy, civic virtues, and workplace behavior.

But wait: Civic engagement and democratic behaviors may be applicable to largely white middle- and upper-middle-income schools in suburbs and small towns, but what about the ghettos and barrios in New York, Chicago, Compton (California), and Houston, where so many schools have poor and minority students? After all, anyone here in this audience could easily say that low-paying jobs, lack of health insurance, inadequate housing, and residential segregation make a mockery of cultivating civic engagement in ghettos. What urban students need, many would say, is basic literacy, not civic-mindedness. And I would reply that the two are joined at the hip. The skills of reading, writing, math, and reasoning are the cognitive building blocks of civic literacy and engagement.[25]

Becoming literate is exactly what poor, immigrant, and non-English-speaking parents want most dearly for their children. It is also what most teachers and employers want. Basic literacy contains intellectual tools for children to gain a deeper understanding of themselves, their immediate surroundings, the workplace, and the society in which they have been born and reared. And there are in-school strategies that can make literacy happen. Some districts establish programs that prevent students from falling behind academically (e.g., preschool, nongraded primary units), interventions throughout a student's career in school (e.g., special programs for identified students falling behind academically), and remediation (e.g., one-on-one tutoring). The overarching purpose of these strategies is for students to acquire basic literacy and convert that literacy into civic engagement each day of a child's life in classrooms and schools, not for some future job.[26]

But that is a tall order. For decades, urban schools have endured malign neglect in resources. Corporate, civic, and educational leaders, using the rhetoric of "all children can learn" and promising equal access, have raised academic standards, established a uniform curriculum, and told teachers and students to work harder at boosting academic achievement. Such leaders, rather than ensuring that all urban children are healthy, adequately housed, and prepared for kindergarten, send a clear message to urban practitioners and students: Stop whining, pull your socks up, and do well on tests.[27]

Where my utopian inclinations may show is in expecting national and state officials and business leaders to support sharp increases in federal and state funding for urban schools; attack poverty through a higher minimum wage, full employment, and health insurance for the uninsured; and construct a national children's policy that knits together education, community development, child care, nutrition, housing, and other social services. Seeing urban school reform as community-wide engagement is uncommon among most current policymakers.

There are, however, some urban mayors who not only believe that better public schools will make cities livable places for young families but work toward that end. While a political revolution does not appear to be on the horizon, incremental improvements are still valuable even after September 11th when education has largely fallen off the nation's agenda and a stumbling economy has meant cuts in state and local education budgets. There is no sin in tinkering toward utopia as long as you know where you are going.[28]

Let me sum up my answers to the question of how to get more "good" schools in the form of directions to take rather than detailed prescriptions for action:

- Pursue civic engagement as the primary purpose of tax-supported public schooling.
- Respond to clear differences among students and schools by allocating resources unequally while pursuing reforms inside and outside of schools.
- Encourage local autonomy and parental choice among public schools yet hold all schools to the three criteria of goodness described earlier.

These are my answers to the question of how to get more "good" schools. What I propose, of course, is out of sync politically with current trends of state and federal accumulation of authority over local schools and widespread standardizing of local curriculum, management, and organization. What I propose is also out of sync with current reform thinking that urban schools alone can raise academic achievement. After all, 80% of a child's time is spent at home and in the neighborhood, not in school. To simply state this stubborn fact is not to provide an alibi for schools that do little to improve student performance; it merely re-states the obvious that focusing only on the student assumes that all that needs to be done must occur only in the school itself. Improving urban schools requires linked educational, political, economic, and social reform.

Out of sync as I may be with present trends, some hopeful signs suggest a possible meltdown in the present one-best-school ideology. Beginning in the late 1960s, driven by desegregation court decisions, alternative programs were established that ranged from highly traditional to intensely progressive to hybrids of both. From these efforts, a small body of evidence has grown to demonstrate positive linkages between desegregation and academic achievement. Because parents could choose which schools to send their children to, no official approval or disapproval was stamped on these alternatives.[29]

Since then, alternative schools anchored in the principle of parental choice have survived and, in the early 1990s, expanded into the charter school movement. Over 2,100 public charter schools of different ideologies embracing traditional, progressive, community-based, and democratic purposes have been approved by state and local boards. Moreover, the small-schools movement, aimed primarily at high schools, the most traditional of the age-graded levels, has also slowly broadened the range of "good" schools, particularly in big cities.[30]

Furthermore, the federal government has displayed a born-again acceptance of different versions of "good" schools. The federally funded Comprehensive School Reform Demonstration program has authorized $150 million for states and districts to improve schools by choosing among a menu of existing school-site programs. These efforts, however, are tied primarily to test-score improvement. [31]

These are hopeful signs but I am far from confident that a meltdown in the doctrinaire one-best-school idea is about to begin. Evidence of social stratification in charter schools replicating the segregation occurring in the larger society suggests that public school choice alone is far from a satisfactory solution. Moreover, American schools are even more racially and ethnically segregated than they were two decades ago.[32]

Much social and economic reform outside of schools needs to be done in tandem with in-school reforms to get at the sources of the test-score gap between white and minority students and high percentages of families and children in poverty. Studies do show that decreasing poverty has had a positive impact on test scores. Historical efforts by unions to engage working-class citizens in school affairs and contemporary efforts to get lower-income groups out to vote on school issues suggest out-of-school movements that can impact urban and rural schools mired in poverty. Current efforts in suing states to secure more funding for schools enrolling low-income minority children, expanding federal housing vouchers to let poor families relocate to suburbs, and providing adequately paying jobs for the working poor are only a few out-of-school initiatives that need public support and collective political action.[33]

Parents, practitioners, policymakers, and educators who worry about the current orthodoxy of a one-best-school and question whether the goal of equal access to academic knowledge is sufficient for urban schools might mobilize political support for reforms inside and outside of public schools.

Am I utopian about such matters? Maybe. But I have learned after almost five decades of working in and around public schools that what really matters is not a loophole-free guarantee of reform success but individuals deciding to work collectively for something that is worthwhile. And restoring the centrality of civic engagement to American public schools, generating diversity in "good" schools, and reducing social and academic inequities in urban schools are, indeed, worthwhile acts.

4

Reflections

Preparing these lectures dredged up some personal and professional dilemmas that I have wrestled with for decades.[1] As I wrote out my lectures, issues arose again and again that I had had to face as a teacher, administrator, researcher, parent, and taxpayer.

In this final chapter I distill the argument that I advanced in the three lectures and then move to exploring these durable dilemmas that are deeply entangled in my analysis and proposals. I offer these reflections because my contacts with tens of thousands of practitioners, policymakers, researchers, and graduate students over the years have convinced me that that I am not alone in struggling with these thorny dilemmas. By openly discussing these value conflicts, I hope that readers will be equally frank with themselves and colleagues in working through the inevitable compromises that each of us must fashion as we muddle toward the kinds of "good" schooling that we seek for children.

THE FUNDAMENTAL ARGUMENT OF THE BOOK

Twice in the last century, business-driven coalitions of corporate and union leaders, public officials, and parents have drafted educators into reforming public schools. Between the 1880s and 1930s and the 1980s and 2002, these reformers substantially altered school governance, organization, management, and curriculum to make public schools a virtual arm of the economy. Although they had much less influence on modifying routine teaching practices in these two periods of school reform, their influence was sufficiently pervasive to create an educational orthodoxy of a one-best-school. In the late 19th century, diverse bands of progressives engineered the transformation of larger, politically appointed school boards to smaller ones where local business and professional leaders picked trained superintendents to manage districts and schools. Other progressives sought to prepare students for the industrialized workplace through student-centered curriculum and instruction in both academic and vocational studies. What emerged from these progressive innovations was the rhetoric and policy of a one-best system of schooling that reigned as educational orthodoxy until the 1970s.

Not until the late 20th century did another corporate-inspired reform coalition dominate educational rhetoric and policy. Beginning in the early 1980s, reformers, working aggressively through federal and state officials, slowly but passionately began to apply business principles to the practice of schooling at the district and local school through standards-based reform, massive testing, and holding educators and students accountable for results. Reformers believed that high academic standards, tests, and accountability would open doors in the competitive economy for all students, but especially minorities. The beliefs were captured in the slogan "All children can learn."

By the beginning of the 21st century, this business-inspired coalition of reformers had created another orthodoxy of a uniform one-best-school for the nation. The current version of a one-best-school has strengthened, embellished, and glamorized the traditional model of a "good" public school. That model is the historic age-graded school with a standardized curriculum and uniform teaching practices that prepare both urban and suburban students for tests with dire consequences for those who fail.

The present educational orthodoxy is bad for American schools for the following reasons. First, the popular purpose of preparing students for an information-based workplace has largely overwhelmed the fundamental purpose of tax-supported public schooling in a democracy: building literate, civic-minded, socially responsible students who prize productive labor.

Second, the theory behind using schools to bolster the economy is seriously flawed by the absence of credible evidence that students who pass tests and finish high school then get admitted to and graduate from college, obtain high-paying jobs, and perform well in those positions.

Third, the nurturing of a one-best-school that is consistent with a traditional education as "good" for all students ignores the inevitable student variation in motivation, interests, and capabilities. Further, a one-best-school model disregards the historic diversity of "good" schools. Over the past century, there have been traditional, progressive, community-based, and democratic "good" schools—and hybrids of them—that have served well the varied ends which parents and taxpayers have sought.

Finally, the very core of the contemporary educational orthodoxy that calls for color-blind, class-blind equal treatment places the entire burden for achieving success on the individual student and the school while ignoring structural inequalities (e.g., poverty, segregated housing) that seriously affect families, children, and, inexorably, schools.

In light of these reasons, different kinds of "good" schools and external social reforms are needed more than ever to embrace the full range of social, economic, political, and private purposes public schools are expected to serve. Diverse "good" schools are essential to correct the imbalance in purposes from the present dominance of training for the workplace and increasing an individual's social mobility to one where civic engagement is primary. External social reforms are needed to target those structural inequities that have large effects on families and the schools to which they send their sons and daughters.

To say what ought to be done doesn't get the job done. So how do educators, public officials, corporate leaders, and parents get more "good" schools beyond the current model? The initial task is to ask, "good" for what? The question gets at the competing purposes for public schools and how to braid together civic-mindedness, an appreciation for productive labor, and the highly personal search for success that drives so many families' sons and daughters.

Another question that must be asked is "good" for whom. This gets at the equal-treatment version of educational equality in which a child does not advance to the next grade until he or she meets the academic standard, that is, passes the test. Although equal treatment—the reigning metaphor is a race with everyone at the same starting line—is a thoroughly American version of equality, a competing definition is to help those who need special assistance to get up to the starting line.

This latter version of equality—leveling the playing field—requires in-school programs that prevent students, especially in poor, minority sites, from falling behind academically, such as preschools, nongraded primary units, special programs for those falling behind academically in elementary school, and one-on-one tutoring for those who are furthest behind. This three-pronged in-school strategy requires far more funds than currently are allocated by states to districts enrolling high percentages of low-income students.

Securing higher levels of funding to level the playing field also calls for parents, taxpayers, educators, and researchers to join out-of-school reformers and engage in collective political action. Direct action includes constructing and lobbying for a coherent national children's policy aimed at bringing together local, state, and federal resources to concentrate on helping the whole child in and out of school. Another way is to sue governors and legislatures to provide more funds for poor children. These efforts require sustained collective action at the mayor's office and the state capital, and in Washington, DC.

Other out-of-school strategies include increasing job training for out-of-work parents, raising minimum wages for the working poor, ending discriminatory mortgage practices, expanding federal housing vouchers to give options for low-income families to move out of slums, and providing health insurance coverage for the same families. All of these require concerted and long-term political action. These out-of-school strategies targeting low-income families help children who carry their indirect but important benefits into classrooms, bringing a measure of justice to the phrase "equal opportunity."

Even after answering the questions "good" for what and "good" for whom, there would still remain the sticky issue of knowing whether a particular school is, indeed, "good." When there is a one-best-school model, the judgment of "goodness" is straightforward: How well does the school in question fit the model? But, as I have argued, when there are diverse models of "good" schools and diverse purposes for public schools in a democracy, how can you tell if a school is "good"?

Drawing from the history of public schools and their multiple purposes, I proposed three criteria to be used by students, parents, taxpayers, practitioners, policymakers, and researchers to judge the "goodness" of a school.

- Are parents, staff, and students satisfied with what occurs in the school?
- Is the school achieving the explicit goals that it has set for itself?
- Are democratic behaviors, values, and attitudes evident in the students?

These criteria argue for trusting educators, parents, and students to make the right choices in setting and assessing school goals. School autonomy and public accountability for goals that include the core purpose of public schools—civic engagement—become the criteria to judge the "goodness" of a school.

I ended the lectures with questions aimed at analyzing the strengths and shortcomings of the proposals. In raising these questions, I returned again to those personal dilemmas that I have faced in my own journey these five decades in education and that accompany my loving critique of public schools. And it is to those conflicts that I now turn.

NEGOTIATING DURABLE DILEMMAS

Two dilemmas, in particular, have provoked in me much conflict and thought over the years: Should I work inside or outside schools to improve the lives of my students? Which school reforms have the most payoff for students who are least well off in our society?

Should I work inside or outside schools to improve the lives of my students? Because I was the first member of my family to go to college, becoming a credentialed teacher in 1955 was a big deal. I applied for social studies positions (history was my undergraduate major) in Los Angeles and my home town of Pittsburgh. Both personnel directors rejected me. I eventually got a temporary job teaching biology (my undergraduate minor) in McKeesport Technical High School outside of Pittsburgh. The next year I landed a social studies job in Cleveland (Ohio) the day before Labor Day, convincing me that I was at the bottom of some list of applicants for teaching. Assigned to Glenville High School, a largely black high school on the de facto segregated east side of the city, I taught social studies there for 7 years. Glenville fulfilled my deepest values about doing work that is socially worthwhile and that could help young people see a more promising future than daily life in a ghetto offered. In the late 1950s, the civil rights movement touched our school directly when a group of teachers and students went to hear Martin Luther King, Jr. speak at local churches. The energy and sheer righteousness of the appeal swept over all of us listening to Reverend King speak of the Montgomery bus boycott.

Strong feelings to do something more than teach textbook American history to my six classes a day led me to graduate study in what was then called Negro history and to produce classroom history materials. Eventually, I compiled those materials into my first book. Those feelings also triggered thoughts about working in other organizations rather than teaching. Those thoughts grew stronger as the civil rights protests spread across the South, particularly with the Birmingham (Alabama) marches and the horrific church bombings that occurred in that city.

When I was offered a post teaching history at a college—I had just passed my doctoral orals in history at Case Western Reserve University—I turned down the offer and decided to stay in public schools but do more than teach five classes a day. I accepted a job in Washington, DC, in 1963 as a master teacher of history in an all-black high school where a new program was launched to prepare returning Peace Corps volunteers to become credentialed teachers while they worked in the all-black Cardozo community.

During the 4 years I spent at Cardozo High School as a teacher and later director of the program and the subsequent 5 years that I spent as a teacher and central office administrator in Washington, DC, I came to realize how incredibly naïve I was about school reform. I, and many others who then shared the same convictions, believed that bright, young, idealistic, and energetic teachers who worked in both the school and the community could

make deep academic and social changes in our students, our racially isolated school, and our neighborhood.

I make no apologies for that innocence since it was precisely that innocence which fueled an incredible array of programs seldom seen in the
schools in which we worked. I did see hard-working, inspired teachers,
administrators, and parents working together create for a few years classrooms and schools where poor minority students achieved beyond the
dreams of even those in the schools. These classrooms and schools, sadly,
were the exceptions.

I slowly came to realize the magnitude of the problems of institutional
racism and structural inequalities that faced schools located in racially and
ethnically segregated communities and the enormous leaps in collective
action that would have to be taken by policymakers and ordinary folks to
improve teaching and learning, much less the entire community. As the real-
ization seeped into my thinking, fits of depression laced with a severe self-
questioning about my roles as teacher and administrator, in addition to
being a white man in largely black schools, wracked me. I considered seriously leaving a job I loved to work for change outside of schools.[2]

I wrestled with the dilemma for a few years and after an ill-chosen
sojourn of 6 months at the U.S. Commission on Civil Rights, I returned to
the public school work to continue working within schools as a teacher, later
as a superintendent, and eventually as a researcher. Whether my career choices emerged from a lack of courage and conviction, an abiding awareness of
my responsibilities to my growing family, my love for classroom teaching, or
a growing humility about what I could achieve and the worth of even those
small victories, or some mix of all of these, I do not know. What remained
with me, however, was the hard nugget of truth—some academics might
label it a theory of action—that sustained academic improvement of poor
minority students coming from ghetto communities required joint work in
both school and community. That deep understanding extracted from my
work at Glenville and Cardozo never left me even as I concluded that I could
not do both full-time and chose to continue working in schools.[3]

Thus, these lectures contain insights I derived from my work as a practitioner. Within a school system, for example, political and organizational
factors had to be addressed to alter taken-for-granted commonplaces such as
the age-graded school, how resources were allocated to reach prized goals,
and the uses of power to help those whose voices too often went unheard.
Also, well-grounded political and social theory explained for me the interac-
tion between schools and society. Political power underscored the themes of
institutional vulnerability of schools to external forces (e.g., business-led
reform coalitions, social movements, political groups lobbying for curricular
changes) and larger social issues that historically and persistently shaped

school practices such as poverty, racial discrimination, structural inequities, and under-funded urban schools.

These political and organizational insights extracted from daily experiences also gave me a theoretical basis on which to judge reforms. Current state and federal strategies of placing the full burden on schools and schools alone—the orthodoxy of a one-best-school for all students—to remedy low academic performance is, at best, inadequate and, at worst, willfully blind to a history filled with examples of reform-minded elites expecting schools to solve severe social problems and then blaming students, teachers, and administrators for failing to remedy those very same problems.

These themes extracted from my practical experiences in urban schools as a teacher and administrator, then, led to my basic decision to join internal and external reforms to improve students' and their families' lives. But which reforms have the greatest payoff for students and their families? That question involves the second dilemma with which I have struggled.

Which school reforms have the most payoff for students who are least well off in our society? Let me set matters straight quickly: no one knows for sure. Scientific studies cannot establish the "best" reform because reforming schools is essentially a series of political acts, not technical solutions to problems. Think about the list of reforms proposed to reduce the test-score gap between whites and poor minorities.

- Helping poor minority families will increase their income through steady work at livable wages; their children's test scores will improve.
- Moving families out of slums into suburbs where economic and educational opportunities are available will lead to their children's increased academic achievement.
- Providing research-proven reading programs for every single poor minority child will produce test score gains.
- Concentrated test preparation for low-scoring students will raise test scores.
- Giving each child a laptop computer will motivate students to learn more, faster, and better.

The proposed reforms are endless and uncertain in their outcomes. The values embedded in these proposals are a matter of faith, not scientific findings. Deciding which ones to adopt generates fierce struggles over the "best" reforms. These battles, I have learned, are about power, control, and access to resources. If that is the case, as I believe it is, then how can policy and personal choices about reform strategies be made?

For me, the answer is to have bifocal vision: Look for both collective and individual action. School and district improvements require collective pursuit of social, economic, and political changes inside and outside schools. For the individual, drawing from one's experiences, moral values, knowledge, skills, and deciding, on the basis of what resources are available, which principles matter the most and then determining where one should place his or her bets is what I propose.

My conflict embedded in the above question is simply stated: How much I should trust my direct experiences and how much I should trust what I have learned from observation, listening, and research. This is not an either/or matter since both come into play but I have found again and again in making decisions as a teacher, administrator, and researcher an edgy tension over which knowledge I trust the most. Because constraints of time often require decisions based on partial information, figuring out which of these values take precedence in a particular situation has left me tense and conflicted.

Let me be more precise. Many of my values about which reforms make the most sense and should be implemented derive from my years in urban schools as a teacher, teacher educator, director of staff development, and superintendent. From these experiences, I am continually tempted to focus on only those reforms that improve the lot of the classroom teacher who is the ultimate insider when it comes to putting reforms into practice and the primary gatekeeper to student learning. Yet teacher voices have been largely unheard in policymaking circles. Many of my writings and speeches over the decades have been, to put a charitable spin on it, teacher-centric. So I have had to consider often, especially as a researcher who has studied a vast array of attempted school reforms in cities and suburbs (e.g., literature of Effective Schools and systemic reform), that other approaches are promising also. The tension between trusting experience-produced knowledge and trusting research-produced knowledge is one that has haunted me for years. I swivel back and forth between the two poles, forging compromises again and again for those practitioners, policymakers, and researchers who ask for my recommendations. And that is certainly the case in these lectures. Three personal examples may help clarify the point.

My experience in urban schools tells me over and over that the school alone cannot achieve the high academic standards and personal, social, and economic goals that parents, policymakers, and practitioners seek. The inside/outside dual strategy of urban school reform recognizes that experience-produced truth.

I recall, for example, when I served as a superintendent that the school board's and superintendent's unrelenting concentration on improving academic performance in low-achieving schools with large numbers of poor and language-minority students paid off with higher test scores in elementary schools. I also learned that having a range of alternative schools was essential in order to meet the diversity of family and student needs.

Toward the end of my superintendency, I scheduled a conference with a mother and father who were in obvious distress. Of their three children, one was in one of our regular elementary schools, another was in a full-day special education program, and the third was doing badly in one of the district's three high schools. The parents, both of whom had been harsh critics of school board policies providing alternative schools and of me personally for expanding alternatives, asked if there was space in our small alternative high school, one that they had often attacked in letters to the editor of the local paper and at board meetings. The school prided itself on giving students choice in constructing their own daily schedules, working on projects, and calling teachers by their first names—practices these parents personally scorned. Their son wanted to attend this school. In light of their scorching criticism of the program and personal attacks on me and school board members, it must have been very difficult for them to swallow their political convictions and ask for help from the very person they were intent on removing from office. After I confirmed that space was available, the young man eventually attended our alternative high school. Nothing more had to be said between me and the tormented parents about how in one family with three children the school board was far-sighted enough—and the tax base was sufficiently deep—to provide options for all three children.

The tax base in my district reveals another truth that comes from direct experience and has shaped my choice of reforms. Money matters and it matters a great deal in urban schools.

Adequate funding is a fundamental prior condition for school improvement. Urban schools have been historically under-funded. Although researchers argue among themselves whether spending money yields increases in academic achievement, I know from direct experience—not research—that schools with large classes with many unqualified teachers and out-of-date textbooks and under-equipped science labs and leaky roofs need large infusions of money to reduce class size, hire qualified and experienced teachers, modernize science labs, and mend buildings. None of this yet refers to providing diverse curriculum and materials for the 30 students per class whose academic and social needs vary. Only someone who has avoided spending substantial time in an urban school can say money is unimportant.[4]

Yet increasing funding for urban schools to provide more preschool education and early interventions to prevent students' reading and math deficits from piling up, securing qualified teachers, reorganizing the age-graded school, and reducing class size are political acts of fairness. The political acts require, among other things, mobilizing different constituencies across a district and a state to lobby the legislature and governor and enticing voters to open their pocketbooks to increase appropriations for underfunded urban schools. Another political strategy is to sue the state on grounds that it fails to provide the constitutional guarantee of an "adequate" or "sound, basic" education. Both efforts seek to bring under-funded urban schools up to the level of better-funded, mostly white suburban schools. It is the quest for political fairness that fuels such reform strategies.[5]

My final example concerns reform strategies within districts. When I was superintendent for 7 years in the 1970s in Arlington (Virginia), the school board and I launched a top-down strategy of demanding from individual schools concerted efforts to reach five goals, including higher academic achievement. We were concerned about how major demographic changes in enrollment of minority students, especially those whose native language was not English, had led to less community confidence in the district's ability to continue its previous enviable record of high academic achievement and being an attractive district to parents.

The school board set in motion a process of clear and specific demands that the superintendent and his lieutenants implemented. We aligned our five goals with district curriculum and state tests. Principals and teachers were evaluated, in part, on reaching their school and classroom goals, ones that were expected to be consistent with those of the district. We provided much help to schools through additional resources, coaching, and a broad array of professional-development opportunities focused on the five district goals. We made sure to explain and clarify our district strategy to parents, community groups, and students about the changes we expected to be put into practice. We published annual reports of academic and nonacademic progress, school by school. I closely monitored principals in the 35-plus schools in the district.

I spent a day a week in schools each year of my superintendency and met with every single principal twice a year to assess their school goals and to evaluate their performance. When improvements failed to materialize, there were explicit consequences for those schools. A few principals were demoted or fired. A few principals who were ambitious, skillful at their work, and continually achieved their school's goals were promoted to continue districtwide efforts. For better or worse, I became a highly visible superintendent in schools and classrooms, fought for more alternatives for parents, and thoroughly identified with improving instructional outcomes for all students.

And improvements in the system occurred. We displayed annual data that confirmed the progress that our students had made in reaching the five goals, especially improvements in mandated state test scores—except for the gap between minorities and white students, especially at the secondary level.

While both white and minority scores rose, the gap persisted.

Based on these experiences in a small city, I have been partial to district efforts to expand alternatives for parents while improving academic achievement. Yet that bias toward district-wide and systemic reforms has not obscured the abject failure in many districts, including Washington, DC, where I directed a system-wide professional-development program. I know well about district failures. Still the occasional district success story captures my attention and renews my confidence that just the right fragile mix of superintendent and school board leadership, a clear mission, sufficient local talent in schools and classrooms, adequate resources, support from union and civic and business leadership, and the development of an instructional infrastructure to support the mission can make a difference in students' academic and nonacademic lives.[6]

So, as a researcher, I have sought out and studied those districts that seemingly possess those essential governance, organizational, managerial, and instructional features. Had I been a state official or active in state-wide school reforms, I might well have decided that the state was the best unit of school reform, not the district. Again, the tension between trusting the knowledge derived from direct experiences and research-produced knowledge comes into play.[7]

CONCLUSIONS

These examples of how I have tried to reconcile the conflicting values about which forms of knowledge to trust in devoting my energies to pursuing particular reform strategies bring me to the end of my reflections.

I offered these thoughts on the lectures and the dilemmas with which I have wrestled these many years in the hope that others who have had similar experiences or were curious about my intellectual and personal journey might gain insights into their own careers as educators. What emerges clearly for me is how my experiences as a teacher and the values inherent to teaching practice, seasoned considerably by intellectually re-working (again and again) those experiences in my writing and later research, substantially shaped my later choices as a district-based teacher educator, superintendent, and professor.

Being a practitioner these many decades engaged me in a form of reasoning that grew out of each context I found myself in. I improvised to tailor my actions to the unique situations I faced. My theories of action resulting from these prior experiences and reflections on those experiences, shaped by my work as a classroom, school, and district practitioner, spilled over to my choices and my work as a researcher. This is not a stunning insight, to be sure, yet it helps me explain to myself how deeply teaching in urban schools has affected me and to understand the inescapable dilemmas that accompany that act of teaching.

Too often academics and policymakers underestimate the power of practice in shaping one's theories of action or see practice as an atheoretical stumbling from one gimmick to another, forsaking a deeper understanding of one's work. That has not been the case for me or for many teachers and administrators with whom I have worked these many years. I offered these reflections as testimony to the wisdom of practice that each of us can extract from our practitioner experiences as we muddle through the inescapable conflicts that arise from our work.[8]

Notes

Introduction

1. Another reason that I put the word in quotation marks is to make clear that it is a value judgment based on personal conceptions of "goodness" in schools. Any conception of a "good" school is anchored in each of our experiences and values about what we believe are the purposes of schooling in a democracy, what knowledge is of most worth, how learning and teaching should occur, and what constitutes school success. In the chapters that follow, I elaborate on different versions of "good" schools and argue why such diversity is essential in public schools within a democracy.

Chapter 1

1. Quoted in Herbert Kliebard, *Schooled to Work: Vocationalism and the American Curriculum, 1876–1946* (1999), p. 29.

2. Ad appearing in *The New York Times Magazine*, April 28, 1991, p. 21.

3. "Text of President Bush's State of the Union Address to Congress," *The New York Times*, January 30, 2002, p. A22.

4. "Text of Levy's Remarks on Overhauling Staff," *The New York Times*, August 8, 2001.

5. Mark A. Smith, *American Business and Political Power* (2000); Robert Wiebe, *Businessmen and Reform: A Study of the Progressive Movement* (1962); Samuel Bowles and Herbert Gintis, *Schooling in Capitalist America: Educational Reform and the Contradictions of Economic Life* (1976); Charles Lindblom, *Politics and Markets: The World's Political-Economic Systems* (1977).

The historiographical literature is split on the point of the establishment and growth of tax-supported public schools in the 19th century. The initial story was crafted by early 20th-century progressive reformers who saw the public schools as part of the larger pageant of progress in a democratic society. Ellwood P. Cubberley and other reformers constructed their accounts of the growth of public schools along those lines (see Cubberley, *Public Education in the United States*, 1919). A subsequent generation of scholars argued that business elites imposed schools on the growing working class largely composed of immigrants and migrants to maintain a stable political regime and social order. See Michael Katz, *The Irony of Early School Reform* (1968); Joel Spring, *Education and the Rise of the Corporate State* (1975); and Bowles and Gintis (1976). Those historians who wrote from similar vantage points were labeled revisionists. The issue of elites' imposing schools on a passive working class has been challenged by Julia Wrigley, *Class Politics and Public Schools, Chicago, 1900–1950* (1982); Ira Katznelson and Margaret Weir, *Schooling for All: Class, Race, and the Decline of the Democratic Ideal* (1985); David Hogan, *Class and Reform: School and Society in Chicago, 1880–1930* (1985); and others. Diane Ravitch has countered the elites' social control impulse with an argument that public schools arose from a genuine democratic impulse to educate Americans (meaning, in the 19th century, white boys and girls); see *The Troubled Crusade* (1983). She also attacked the revisionists in *Revisionists Revised: A Critique of the Radical Attack on the Schools* (1978). A third view combines the polar opposites and adds an organizational and political perspective to account for the growth of bureaucracies in school districts and the compromises that reformers constructed during the progressive era, the post–World War II years, and the closing decades of the 20th century. See Selwyn Troen, *The Public and The Schools: Shaping the St. Louis System, 1838–1920* (1975). For succinct but different renderings of this historiography, see Katznelson and Weir, (1985), pp. 10–27, 91–93, 99–103, and 210–222; and Jeffrey Mirel, *The Rise and Fall of an Urban School System, Detroit, 1907–1981* (1993), pp.vii–xiii.

6. For a discussion of manual training, see Lawrence Cremin, *The Transformation of the School* (1961), pp. 24–34; Marvin Lazerson, *Origins of the Urban School: Public Education in Massachusetts, 1870–1915* (1971), chs. 3–6; Harvey Kantor, "Vocationalism in American Education: The Economic and Political Context, 1880–1930" (1982), pp. 14–44; Dorothy Shipps, "Corporate Influence on Chicago School Reform" (1998), pp. 161–183. For a recent example of corporate largess, see Kate Zernike, "Pupils Prosper From an Investment" (2000, August 2), p. A11. Investment house Merrill Lynch chose 251 first graders at random in 10 cities' tough neighborhoods in 1988 and now over 90% of those who graduated high school will receive scholarships paying all expenses for 4 years at the college they enrolled in.

7. For the origins and development of the age-graded school, see David Angus, Jeffrey Mirel, and Maris Vinovskis, "Historical Development of Age Stratification in Schooling" (1988), pp. 213–236.

8. Marvin Lazerson and W. Norton Grubb (Eds.), *American Education and Vocationalism: Documents in Vocational Education, 1870-1970* (1971). For union involvement in vocational education reform, see Katznelson and Weir (1985), chapter 6.

9. Quoted in Raymond Callahan, *Education and the Cult of Efficiency* (1962), pp. 13–14.

10. Quote cited in Merle Curti, *The Social Ideas of American Educators* (1935), p. 203.

11. Kliebard (1999); Larry Cuban, "Enduring Resiliency: Enacting and Implementing Federal Vocational Education Legislation" (1982), pp. 45–78; Callahan (1962), pp. 12–14; Hogan (1985), pp. 167–174; Paul Peterson, *The Politics of School Reform, 1870–1940* (1985), pp. 65–71; Harvey Kantor, *Learning to Earn: School, Work, and Vocational Reform in California, 1880–1930* (1988).

12. David Tyack, *One Best System* (1974); Callahan (1962); Curti (1935), chapter 6. San Francisco reference comes from Katzelnelson and Weir (1985), p. 95.

13. Tyack (1974), pp. 126–128. I have used Tyack's typology of Progressive reformers (administrative, pedagogical, reconstructionist, etc.). The text refers to the administrative progressives. Also see George Counts, *The Social Composition of Boards of Education* (1927) and Joseph Cronin, *The Control of Urban Schools* (1973).

14. Carol Ray and Roslyn Mickelson, "Business Leaders and the Politics of School Reform," (1990), pp.119–135; Dorothy Shipps, "Echoes of Corporate Influence: Managing Away Urban School Troubles" (2000), pp. 82–106. David Kearns and Denis Doyle, *Winning the Brain Race: A Bold Plan to Make Our Schools Competitive* (1988). Nancy Perry, "Saving the Schools: How Business Can Help" (1988, November 7), pp. 42–46, 50–56.

15. U.S. Commission on Excellence in Education, *A Nation at Risk* (1983). Gordon Lafer maps a sequence of events in the same quarter-century where employers focused on workers' lack of skills and the need for more training and education to equip employees for the future workplace; see *The Job Training Charade* (2002). Also see Michael J. Handel, "Is There a Skills Crisis?" (2000).

16. Stewart Purkey and Marshall Smith, "Effective Schools: A Review" (1983), pp. 427-452; The National Education Goals Panel, *The National Education Goals Report: Building a Nation of Learners* (1995); Jane David and Paul Goren, *Transforming Education: Overcoming Barriers* (1993); Cathie Jo Martin, *Stuck in Neutral: The Business and Politics of Human Capital Investment Policy* (2000), pp. 192–207.

17. Economists and widely respected analysts produced best-sellers in these years that judged schools as failures in teaching students to think and to solve problems. See Ray Marshall and Marc Tucker, *Thinking for a Living: Education and the Wealth of Nations* (1992); Robert Reich, *The Work of Nations* (1991); and Lester Thurow, *Head to Head: The Coming Economic Battle Among Japan, Europe, and America* (1992).

For data that challenge the key assumptions reformers made, see Henry Levin, "Educational Performance Standards and the Economy" (1998), pp. 4–10. Lafer (2002) also argues persuasively that this mismatch-skills thesis, which employers and reformers use to explain the loss in real wages and then justify more training and education, has less evidence to support it then the evidence supporting institutional factors that explain the same wage loss, such as decreased unionization, persistence of gender and race discrimination in the workplace, etc. Also see James Rosenbaum, *Beyond College for All* (2001), chapter 5.

18. The phrase comes from Shipps (2000), p. 89; also see Kearns and Doyle (1988). Dorothy Shipps pointed out that in my argument about business influence in school reform I focus mostly on corporate leaders from major businesses involved in school reform rather than the diversity of small, medium, and large businesses that I describe earlier in the lecture. In effect, I say business leaders were a diverse lot but then concentrate on "Big Business" influence in school reform. This is a fair criticism. What I should have pointed out in the body of the lecture was that small businesses and chambers of commerce were represented nationally by associations (e.g., National Alliance of Business, U.S. Chamber of Commerce) that often shared similar positions on high standards, tests, and accountability as the National Association of Manufacturers, Business Roundtable, and other large corporate associations. Cathie Jo Martin makes a similar point on human resource and training issues; she points out that national associations of small, medium, and large businesses concurred on those policy proposals. See Martin (2000), pp. 194–197.

19. For an in-depth case study of a corporate elite heavily involved in one city's school politics and reform, see Dorothy Shipps, "The Invisible Hand: Big Business and Chicago School Reform"(1997); Roslyn A. Mickelson, "Corporations and Classrooms: A Critical Examination of the Business Agenda for Urban School Reform" (2000), pp. 127–173.

20. Influential educational policymakers had evolved a similar strategy during the 1980s and early 1990s that derived from the strategies used by California State Superintendent Bill Honig between 1983 and 1990. By the early 1990s, this strategy had come to be called "systemic reform" and nicely converged with the market-driven prescriptions for school reform. Currently, 49 states have implemented standards of what their students should know and do and have established tests to assess their performance. The number of states that administer student tests that are aligned with published standards in at least one subject climbed from 35 in 1998 to 41 in 2000. According to *Education Week* (1999, January 11), 27 states rate schools primarily on the basis of test scores; 14 states have authorized their departments of education to close and take over low-performing schools. In 18 states, students who fail the statewide graduation test do not receive diplomas. See Marshall Smith and Jennifer O'Day, "Systemic School Reform" (1990). Also see Maris Vinovskis, *History of Educational Policy Making* (1999), pp. 171–202. For descriptions of actions taken at state and national levels, see *Education Week*, "Quality Counts 1999, Rewarding Results, Punishing Failure" (1999, January 11); Jodi Wilgoren, "For 2000, the G.O.P. Sees Education

in a New Light"(2000, August 2), p. A15; David Sanger, "Bush Pushes Ambitious Education Plan," (2001, January 24), pp. A1, A14.

21. *Education Week*, "Quality Counts 2001" (2001, January 23); Alex Molnar, *Giving Kids the Business: The Commercialization of America's Schools* (1996); Amy Wells, *Time to Choose: America at the Crossroads of School Choice Policy* (1993); Carrie Lips, " 'Edupreneurs': A Survey of For-Profit Education" (2000); Alex Molnar and Joseph Reaves, *"Buy Me! Buy Me!" Fourth Annual Report on Trends in Schoolhouse Commercialism, 2000–2001* (2001).

22. Anne Bradley, "The Business of Reforming Cincinnati's Schools" (1993, May 19), pp. 1, 16; Jay Mathews, "Chief Academic Officers," http://www. - aasa.org/publications/sa/2001_06/mathews_cao.htm; Henry Becker, Jason Ravitz, and YanTien Wong, "Teaching, Learning, and Computing: 1998 National Survey" (1999); Molnar (1996); Mark Walsh, "Ka-Ching! Business Cashing in on Learning" (1999, November 24), pp. 1, 14-16; Constance Hays, "Today's Lesson: Soda Rights" (1999, May 21), pp. C1, C19; Molnar and Reaves (2001).

23. Larry Cuban, *How Teachers Taught*, second edition (1993); Alfie Kohn, "Tests That Cheat Students" (1999, December 9), p. A31; Maureen O'Donnell, "Test Prep Book for 3rd-graders Causes Stir" (2000, September 12).

24. Quoted in Marilyn Cochran-Smith and Mary Kim Fries, "Sticks, Stones, and Ideology: The Discourse of Reform in Teacher Education" (2001), p. 7.

25. Cuban (1993); Arthur Zilversmit, *Changing Schools: Progressive Education Theory and Practice, 1930–1960* (1993).

26. Kearns and Doyle (1988), p. 28. See also Gordon Lafer's critique of skills deficits among today's workers including employer surveys and quotes (2002).

27. Labaree (1997); Doyle (2000), p. 27; Kohn (1999); O'Donnell (2000).

28. Jeannie Oakes, Karen Quartz, Steve Ryan, and Martin Lipton, *Becoming Good American Schools: The Struggle for Civic Virtue in Education Reform* (2000); Denise Gelberg, *The "Business" of Reforming American Schools* (1997).

29. Although teachers' anecdotal reports make this point repeatedly, few researchers have systematically investigated it. One who has is Norton Grubb, "Dick and Jane at Work: The New Vocationalism and Occupational Literacy Programs," in G. Hall (Ed.), *Changing Work, Changing Workers* (1997), pp. 159–188.

30. I found the analysis and data offered by Smith (2000) convincing. He argues that on issues that unify the business community (e.g., the need for more skilled and knowledgeable workers), businesses heed public opinion polls and election results in shaping their positions, making political contributions, and lobbying for legislation (see chapters 4–6). Specific instances of private-sector responsiveness after resistance can be seen in business opposition to water and air pollution legislation and other environmental issues in the 1970s.

31. John Sipple, "Institutional Constraints on Business Involvement in K–12 Education Policy" (1999), pp. 447–488.

32. How business agendas for public schools were curtailed by labor unions in Chicago can be seen in Julia Wrigley, *Class Politics and Public Schools, Chicago 1900-1950* (1982). See also Katznelson and Weir (1985), chapter 6.

33. Abby Goodnough, "For Levy, Can-Do Business Style Runs into Education Reality" (2001, April 9). See also Mickelson (2000), pp. 140–144.

34. In 2002, President George W. Bush signed legislation called "No Child Left Behind." The reauthorized Elementary and Secondary Education Act, among many provisions, mandated that any district receiving federal funds had to annually test students between third and eighth grades (http://www.-ed.gov/offices/OESE/esea/).

35. Larry Cuban, "The Media and Polls on Education—Over the Years" (1998), pp. 69-82. In 2000, over 60% of public school parents said that it was more important to "prepare students for college or work" than to "prepare students for effective citizenship." See Lowell Rose and Alec Gallup, "The 32nd Annual Phi Delta Kappa/Gallup Poll of the Public's Attitudes Toward the Public Schools" (2000, September), p. 48. The concept of "real schools" comes from John Meyer's and Brian Rowan's work on the power of social beliefs in education and Mary Metz's application of their work to schools. See John W. Meyer and Brian Rowan, "Institutionalized Organizations: Formal Structure as Myth and Ceremony" (1977), pp. 340–363; and Mary Hayward Metz, "Real School: A Universal Drama amid Disparate Experience," in D. Mitchell and M. Goertz (Eds.), *Education Politics for the New Century* (1990), pp. 75–91.

36. Labaree, "Public Goods, Private Goods: The American Struggle over Educational Goals" (1997), pp. 39–81.

37. Kliebard (1986).

38. A few districts have built elaborate instructional and professional-development infrastructures over a number of years and standardized test scores have improved. One has to look carefully at the evidence and disentangle many factors to determine whether the infrastructures led to test score improvements. See Richard Elmore and Diane Burney, *Continuous Improvement in Community District #2, New York City* (1998); and Amy Hightower, "San Diego's Big Boom: District Bureaucracy Meets Culture of Learning" (2001).

39. Levin (1998); and John P. Smith, III, "Tracking the Mathematics of Automobile Production: Are Schools Failing to Prepare Students for Work?" (1999), pp. 835–878. See also Lafer (2002), chapters 2 and 3, for a comprehensive summary of evidence revealing how workplace demands are inconsistent with the theory and beliefs of those who argue for more well-trained graduates from high school and college.

In a synthesis of the differential and unintended effects of high-stakes testing on student learning, two researchers asked if student learning on these consequential tests in 18 states transfer to other commonly used tests (e.g., SAT, NAEP, Advanced Placement). Did test scores go up, go down, or remain stable on these national tests that overlap with the cognitive domains covered in state high stakes tests? The researchers found that in all but one of the national tests, student test scores remained the same or went down after the imposition of state tests carrying high consequences. See Audrey Amrein and David Berliner, "High Stakes Testing, Uncertainty, and Student Learning" (2002).

Critics of using standardized test scores as the only or best indicator of improved teaching and learning have often referred to other important measures that are either ignored or missing because of measurement difficulties. These include quality of intellectual work in school and the linkages between classroom teaching and assessment. The work of Lorrie Shepard is the best in this regard. See "The Contest Between Large-Scale Accountability Testing and Assessment in the Service of Learning: 1970-2001" (2001) and her "The Role of Assessment in a Learning Culture" (1990), pp. 4–14.

Chapter 2

1. Randal Archbold, "What Makes a Good Education?" (2001).

2. In this lecture, I have expanded the argument and evidence from an earlier published chapter. See Larry Cuban, "Why Is It So Hard to Get 'Good' Schools?" (2000), pp. 148–169. For writers who have documented the continuing public battles between traditionalists and progressives in the 19th and 20th centuries see Michael Katz, *Irony of Early School Reform* (1968), pp. 115-160; William Reese, "The Origins of Progressive Education," (2001), pp. 1–24; Diane Ravitch, *Left Back: A Century of Failed School Reforms* (2001). Philip Jackson points out the ancient origins of the ideological struggle over pedagogy and curriculum in *The Practice of Teaching* (1986).

3. I visited both schools in the mid-1980s.

4. This composite is drawn from Leonard Covello, *The Heart Is the Teacher* (1970), pp. xi, 251–254; my work at the Cardozo Project in Urban Teaching in Washington, DC, 1963–1967; and visits to Coalition for Essential Schools and small alternative secondary schools in the San Francisco Bay area in the 1990s.

5. School D is based on descriptions of a Milwaukee (Wisconsin) elementary school called La Escuela Fratney. See Robert Petersen, "La Escuela Fratney," in M. Apple and J. Beane (Eds.), *Democratic Schools* (1995), pp. 58–82; George Wood, *Schools That Work* (1992), pp. 18–25, 36–37, 88–92, 165–167, 260–261.

6. I asked the audience to vote for which of the four "good" schools they would send their children, grandchildren, nephews, and nieces to. I announced that they could vote more than once. Most of the audience voted for school B followed closely by C and D. Out of 200 in the audience, no more than 15 voted for A.

7. Here is a sampling of research on the Eight Year Study (1934–1941), Follow Through evaluation of preschool programs (1967–1971), and reviews of

progressive and traditional approaches to teaching in general and reading in particular: Eugene Smith and Ralph Tyler, *Adventures in American Education, Vol. III: Appraising and Recording Student Progress* (1942); Ernest House, Gene Glass, L. McLean, and D. Walker, "No Simple Answer: Critique of the Follow Through Evaluation" (1978), pp. 128-160; Neville Bennett, *Teaching Styles and Pupil Progress* (1976); Jeanne Chall, *Learning to Read: The Great Debate* (1967).

8. Another example of an equally heated ideological debate is over teacher education in which one side wants to professionalize teaching and the other side wants to deregulate it. The terms of the debate are a series of charges and countercharges that one side is misusing or misstating the research that the other side leans on. See Marilyn Cochran-Smith and Mary Kim Fries, "Sticks, Stones, and Ideology: The Discourse of Reform in Teacher Education" (2001), pp. 3–15.

9. For contemporary accounts, see John Dewey, *School and Society* (1899); Evelyn Dewey and John Dewey, *Schools for Tomorrow* (1915); Harold Rugg and Ann Schumaker, *The Child-Centered School* (1928). For historical accounts, see Lawrence Cremin, *The Transformation of the School* (1961); and Tyack (1974). For a sharply critical view of progressives, see Diane Ravitch, *The Troubled Crusade* (1983) and *Left Back* (2001).

10. For contemporary accounts, see Albert Lynd, *Quackery in the Public Schools* (1953); Arthur Bestor, *Educational Wastelands: The Retreat from Learning in Our Public Schools* (1953); Paul Woodring, *Let's Talk Sense about Our Schools* (1953). For secondary accounts, see Ravitch (1983).

11. For contemporary accounts, see Herbert Kohl, *36 Children* (1967); James Herndon, *The Way It Spozed To Be* (1968); and Nat Hentoff, *Our Children Are Dying* (1966). For histories of this period, see Richard Kluger, *Simple Justice: The History of Brown v. Board of Education and Black America's Struggle for Equality* (1976); and James Patterson, *Brown v. Board of Education: A Civil Rights Milestone And Its Troubled Legacy* (2001).

12. See Chester Finn, *We Must Take Charge: Our Schools and Our Future* (1991); Kearns and Doyle (1988); and E.D. Hirsch, *The Schools That We Need and Why We Don't Have Them* (1996) and publications of the Heritage Foundation and Cato Institute. For neoprogressive approaches to schools, see Fred Newmann and Gary Wehlage, *Successful School Restructuring* (1995). For state policies that show promise in altering traditional ways of teaching math, see David Cohen and Heather Hill, *Learning Policy: When State Education Reform Works* (2001).

13. For this discussion, I rely on George Lakoff, *Moral Politics: What Conservatives Know That Liberals Don't* (1996).

14. David Tyack and Elisabeth Hansot, *Managers of Virtue* (1982); Cremin (1961) and *American Education: The Metropolitan Experience, 1876-1980* (1988); and William Reese, *Power and The Promise of School Reform: Grass-roots Movements During The Progressive Era* (1986).

15. John Meyer, "Reflections on Education as Transcendence" (2000), pp. 206–222.

16. See Stanley Elam (Ed.), *The Gallup/Phi Delta Kappa Polls of Attitudes toward the Public Schools, 1969–1988* (1989). Also see Larry Cuban, "The Media and Polls on Education—Over The Years" (1998), pp. 69–82.

17. For a clear, accessible analysis of the work of the Women's Christian Temperance Union and its Scientific Temperance Instruction campaign in schools, see Jonathan Zimmerman, *Distilling Democracy: Alcohol Education in America's Public Schools, 1880–1925* (1999). The succession of school reforms due to different interest groups' turning to schools to seek redress or some evidence of responsiveness is taken up at length in David Tyack and Larry Cuban, *Tinkering toward Utopia* (1995). See also John Chubb and Terry Moe, *Politics, Markets, and America's Schools* (1990). They argue that "democratic politics" is precisely why schools have become over-bureaucratized, rule-driven, and resistant to change. Each constituency wants something from the schools, and the schools respond by adding another position, another department, another course, another rule, etc. Thus, they conclude, democratic politics has contributed to the growth of school bureaucracies, reluctance to change existing rules and staff, and, ultimately, the failure of public schools to be responsive to parents.

18. For polling data, see Cuban (1998). For common areas between traditionalists and progressives, see Ravitch (2001), pp. 462–464. She points out the commonalities that progressives and traditionalists share: an appreciation for the intellectual heritage that runs from Dewey's concerns for disciplinary-based knowledge to the recent work of Theodore Sizer, Deborah Meier, and Howard Gardner. Similarly, Lauren Resnick maps common ground between the two groups in "The Mismeasure of Learning," (2001), pp. 78–83.

19. In *One Nation, After All* (1998), Alan Wolfe interviewed 200 middle-class Americans (see chapter 1 for methodology and sample). He concluded:

> The two sides presumed to be fighting the culture war do not so much represent a divide between one group of Americans and another as a divide between sets of values important to everyone. People who adhere to such "traditional" values as belief in God, strong families, patriotism, and civic and neighborly loyalty do so because, in most cases, they choose to do so; as awkward as it sounds, they are best described as modern traditionalists. And people who insist on the importance of their own conceptions of God, who value women's autonomy, and who select their friends and neighbors based on personal taste believe strongly in the importance of religion, family, and neighborhood; they can be best viewed as traditional modernists. It is a basic truth of American society that no one is a traditionalist or a modernist, but that everyone lives with varying degrees of both. (p. 279)

20. For a recent example of this centuries-old struggle over defining a "good" school, see Randal C. Archbold, "What Makes a Good Education?" (2001, January 14), p. 27. In this article, at least four different versions of a

"sound, basic education" emerge.

21. Michael Winerip, "Never Mind the Inventive Curriculum. One Test Fits All" (2001, November 18), p. A31. In an earlier decision, Richard Mills had refused to continue a five-year waiver of Regents tests that had been extended to 28 public schools, most of them alternative schools in New York City. Mills ordered that students entering these schools in the fall of 2001 would have to take five Regents exams to graduate. A New York State judge upheld the commissioner's decision to end the waiver. Anemona Hartocollis, "Judge Will Not Allow Schools to Opt Out of Regents Exams" (2001, November 20), p. D3.

22. Williamson M. Evers, an education staffer serving President Bush, said the list of "high-flying schools" that score high on standardized tests and that have at least half of their students both poor and minority prove that accountability alone made the difference. The quote "racist nonsense" comes from Evers. See Richard Rothstein, "An Accountability Push and Fuzzy Math" (2002, April 10), p. A21.

Chapter 3

1. Quoted in Rogers Smith, *Civic Ideals* (1997), p. 217.

2. *Brown v. Board of Education of Topeka*, 347 U.S. 483, 493 (1954).

3. New York State Supreme Court Justice Leland DeGrasse decision, *Campaign for Fiscal Equity et al. v. The State of New York et al.*, 187 Misc.2d1; 719 N.Y.S. 2d 475, January 9, 2001, quoting *Wisconsin v. Yoder*, 406 U.S. 205, 221 (1971), p. 9

4. Michael Rebell, "Education Adequacy, Democracy, and the Courts" (in press); and Helen Ladd and Janet Hansen, *Making Money Matter: Financing America's Schools* (1999).

5. David Labaree, "Public Goods, Private Goods: The American Struggle over Educational Goals" (1997), pp. 39–81.

6. Henry Perkinson, *The Imperfect Panacea: American Faith in Education, 1865–1965* (1968); and Tyack and Cuban (1995).

7. The National Education Goals Panel, *The National Education Goals Report: Building a Nation of Learners, 1995*, p. 11.

8. Robert Hauser, "Should We End Social Promotion? Truth and Consequences" (2001), pp. 151–178. The movement to end social promotion, particularly President Bill Clinton's advocacy of failing students who don't perform up to standards, is also detailed in this chapter. See also Timothy Hacsi, *Children as Pawns: The Politics of Educational Reform* (2002); chapter 4 contains a history of the concept and efforts to stop social promotion since the 1970s.

9. Sarah Deschenes, Larry Cuban, and David Tyack, "Mismatch: Historical

Perspectives on Schools and Students Who Don't Fit Them" (2001), pp. 525–547.

10. Ron Edmonds, "Effective Schools for the Urban Poor" (1979), pp. 18–24; Stuart Purkey and Marshall Smith, "Effective Schools: A Review," (1983), pp. 427–452; Pamela Bullard and Barbara Taylor, *Making School Reform Happen* (1993).

11. Robert Hauser, "Should We End Social Promotion?" (2001).

12. For this section, I rely on an unpublished paper that David Tyack and I wrote in 1988 and that was substantially revised and updated in 2001 by Sarah Deschenes (2001) to examine the standards-based school reform movement. See also Hauser (2001) for states that do indeed mandate early prevention and interventions to lessen later remediation.

13. I found the following sources helpful in thinking through this section. James S. Coleman, "The Concept of Equality of Educational Opportunity" (1968), pp. 7–36; John Rawls, *A Theory of Justice* (1971); John Roemer, *Equality of Opportunity* (1998); Joseph Kahne, *Reframing Educational Policy: Democracy, Community, and the Individual* (1996). I found two articles particularly helpful. They displayed the many meanings of equality as applied to schooling and showed how difficult it is to make any one definition practical at the classroom and school levels. See Christopher Jencks, "Whom Must We Treat Equally for Educational Opportunity to Be Equal?" (1988), pp. 518–533; and David Kirp, "Changing Conceptions of Educational Equity" (1995), pp. 97–112.

14. For a description of opportunity-to-learn standards in the early 1990s, see Wendy Schwartz, "Opportunity to Learn Standards: Their Impact on Urban Students" (1995). The argument against these standards was most concisely put by Albert Shanker in his "Where We Stand" column in the *New York Times* (1993, May 30; paid for by the American Federation of Teachers). He argued that supporters of opportunity-to-learn standards were opposed to new curriculum and assessment standards because so many schools serving low-income populations lack the conditions that make it possible to reach the standards and perform well on the tests. Therefore, these advocates said, establishing these standards and tests is unfair and should wait until the opportunity-to-learn standards have been met. Using many examples, Shanker rebutted this argument by pointing out where high standards are expected for doctors and airline pilots even though all of the conditions for medical school students and wannabe pilots are unequal. The same, he argued, should be the case for schools and students.

15. DeGrasse (2001). See also *Williams et al. v. State of California et al.* (Superior Court, San Francisco (2000).

16. See John Goodlad and Robert Anderson, *The Nongraded Elementary School* (1959); Glen Heathers, "School Organization: Nongrading, Dual Progress, and Team Teaching" (1966), pp. 110–124; B. Frank Brown, *The*

Nongraded High School (1963); Roberto Gutierrez and Robert Slavin, "Achievement Effects of the Nongraded Elementary School: A Best Evidence Synthesis" (1992), pp. 333–376.

17. In 1901, John Dewey noted:

> It is too easy to fall into the habit of regarding the mechanics of school organization … as something comparatively external and indifferent to educational purposes and ideals. We think of grouping children in classes, the arrangement of grades, the machinery by which the course of study is made out and laid down, [and] the method by which it is carried into effect … as, in a way, matters of practical convenience and expediency. We forget that it is precisely such things as these that really control the whole system, even on its distinctively educational side. No matter what is the accepted precept and theory, no matter what the legislation of the school board or the mandate of the school superintendent, the reality of education is found in the personal and face-to-face contact of teacher and child. The conditions that underlie and regulate this contact dominate the educational situation.

Quoted in Herbert Kliebard, *Forging the American Curriculum* (1992), p. 103. For the point that the age-graded school is a powerful social construct embedded in American beliefs about a "good" education, see Meyer and Rowan (1977) and Metz (1990).

18. Jeffrey Pfeffer and Gerald Salancik, *External Control of Organizations* (1978); Frederick Wirt and Michael Kirst, *The Political Dynamics of American Education* (1997).

19. For shared progressive and traditional attitudes on different aspects of schooling, see Stanley Elam (Ed.), *The Gallup/Phi Delta Kappan Polls of Attitudes Toward the Public Schools, 1969–1988* (1988); Ravitch (2001); and Resnick (2001).

20. Robert Putnam argues that contemporary Americans are much less civically engaged than earlier generations. See *Bowling Alone: The Collapse and Revival of American Community* (2000). Presidents G.W. Bush and Clinton repeatedly urged Americans to volunteer in their communities. Clinton established Americorp and his successor, George W. Bush, expanded the initiative. Documenting the disengagement among the young from the larger world and political involvement, prominent Americans have called for service learning and compulsory national service. Former U.S. Senator John Glenn chaired the National Commission on Service-Learning and endorsed elementary and secondary school students' engagement in the community as being as important as academics. Therefore, it should be a regular part of the school day (and annual budget as well). See National Commission on Service-Learning, *Learning in Deed* (2001).

21. DeGrasse, *Campaign for Fiscal Equity* (2001), p. 9.

22. Joseph Kahne and Joel Westheimer, "In Service of What? The Politics of Service Learning" (1996), pp. 592–599; and Joel Westheimer and Joseph Kahne, "Education for Action: Preparing Youth for Participatory Democracy" (2000), pp. 1–20. See also John Dewey, *Democracy and Education* (1916); Amy Gutmann, *Democratic Education* (1987); Benjamin Barber, *A Passion for Democracy* (1998).

23. Smith and Tyler (1942). *Learning in Deed* (2001) calls for the use of multiple measures and portfolios to assess outcomes of students' efforts in the community. Measures of personal cognitive, social, and emotional growth that go beyond academic achievement are available but seldom are adapted for school uses. Participation in community development, arts and humanities projects outside of the schools, voter registration, and similar ventures are other potential measures of a school's success.

24. When economic productivity soared, unemployment decreased, and prosperity thrived in the nation for 8 years in the 1990s, I found no economists, school critics, corporate leaders, or national officials who either pointed to the schools as a causal factor in creating a flourishing economy or gave schools credit for creating the skilled workforce that heightened economic productivity. Instead, the myth of education as a causal link to economic prosperity flourished. For those few writers who questioned the myth, see Clark Kerr, "Is Education Really That Guilty?" (1991, February 7), p. 30; Larry Cuban, "The Corporate Myth of Reforming Public Schools" (1992, October), pp. 157–159; *RAND Institute on Education & Training, Policy Brief,* "Trial by False Fire: Education's Role in U.S. 'Economic Decline" (1994); Levin (1998), pp. 4–10; Valerie Strauss, "When Success Doesn't Add Up" (2000, December 26), p. A12; Larry Cuban, "The Convenient Fallacy of Education" (2001, January 7), pp. P1–2; and Richard Rothstein, "The Blame Game" (2001, March).

25. For example, see the connections made between literacy and civic engagement by Theodore Sizer, *Horace's Compromise: The Dilemma of the American High School* (1984); Amy Gutmann, *Democratic Education* (1987); and Derek Bok, *The Trouble with Government* (2001), pp. 405–407. I found Merle McClung's work on a "civic standard" in his unpublished paper "Citizenship as the Primary Purpose of Public Education" most helpful in thinking through these connections.

26. See the work done in San Diego, 1998–2002, under Superintendent Alan Bersin and Chancellor Anthony Alvarado as documented by Hightower (2001); and Larry Cuban, "Fast and Top-Down: Systemic Reform and Student Achievement in San Diego City Schools" (2002).

27. For data on under-resourced urban schools, see Ladd and Hansen (1999), chapter 9; DeGrasse (2001); Rebell (in press).

28. For recent instances of mayoral takeover of schools, see Gail Chaddock, "Mayors, States Push School Boards Aside," (2002, February 26), p. 1; Michael Kirst and Katrina Bulkley, "'New, Improved' Mayors Take Over City Schools"

(2000, March), pp. 538–546.

29. There is a growing body of evidence on the positive long-term effects of desegregation. See, for example, Amy Stuart Wells and Robert Crain, "Perpetuation Theory and the Long Term Effects of School Desegregation" (1994), pp. 531–555; Amy Wells and Robert Crain, *Stepping Over the Color Line: African-American Students in White Suburban Schools* (1997); The Civil Rights Project, Harvard University, "The Impact of Racial and Ethnic Diversity on Educational Outcomes" (2002). Susan Eaton, *The Other Boston Busing Story: What's Won and Lost Across the Boundary Line* (2002).

30. For charter schools see Bruce Fuller (Ed.), *Inside Charter Schools: The Paradox of Radical Decentralization* (2000). For small schools, see Debra Viadero, "Research: Smaller Is Better" (2001, November 28), pp. 28–30; David Hill, "Breaking Up," (2001, October 10), pp. 34–39.

31. For the federally sponsored effort at school reform, see "The Catalog of School Reform Models," Northwest Regional Educational Laboratory (2001).

32. On resegregation, see Gary Orfield and Nora Gordon, Civil Rights Project, Harvard University, "Schools More Separate: Consequences of a Decade of Resegregation" (2001). See also consequences of public school choice in Stephen Gorard, John Fitz, and Chris Taylor, "School Choice Impacts: What Do We Know?" (2001), pp. 18–23.

33. John A. Powell, Gavin Kearney, and Vina Kay, *In Pursuit of a Dream Deferred: Linking Housing & Education Policy* (2001); Wells and Crain (1997); James Ryan, "Schools, Race, and Money" (1999), pp. 249–316; Smith and O'Day (1990); Linda Jacobson, "Study Links Income Boosts, Academic Success" (2001, November 28), p. 12; and Bok (2001), pp. 324–325, 334–335.

Chapter 4

1. By dilemmas, I mean difficult situations where conflicting values and sizable constraints required me to negotiate a compromise to reduce (but not eliminate) the conflict. These compromises, or what I and others call "satisficing" (that is, I sacrificed in order to satisfy), unraveled eventually and when the situation arose again I had to figure out another way to satisfice. Thus, dilemmas are managed; they are not like problems that are solved once and for all. The concept of dilemma and these distinctions between problems and dilemmas are elaborated and expanded in Larry Cuban, *How Can I Fix It? Finding Solutions and Managing Dilemmas—An Educators' Road Map* (2001).

2. I have written about my experiences at Glenville and Cardozo high schools and as Director of Staff Development in the DC schools in *The Managerial Imperative and the Practice of Leadership in Schools* (1988); see chapters 2 and 4 in that book.

3. Since the introduction of the Master in Arts in Teaching in the mid-1950s

and programs like the Cardozo Project in Urban Teaching, the National Teacher Corps in the 1960s and 1970s, and subsequently Teach for America in the 1980s and 1990s, cadres of young college graduates without teaching credentials have entered mostly urban schools to teach from 1 to 5 years and then depart for other educational positions or other careers. The high attrition rates among these teachers rival the rates among teacher education graduates—both being extraordinarily high for professional occupations. Nonetheless, on balance, experiencing the exhilaration and exhaustion of urban teaching marks these young men and women for life whether they end up as school administrators, lawyers, academics, public officials, or business leaders. In making a profound impression on young people launching careers, urban teaching makes clear the linkage between poverty and schooling, between social inequities and academic achievement. Conceptual abstractions become far more concrete and personal than public officials' pronouncements, pundits' comments or articles in journals.

4. Hacsi (2002), chapter 5; Ladd and Hansen (1999).

5. DeGrasse (2001); Rebell (forthcoming); Ladd and Hansen (1999).

6. See Hess (1999). Michael Usdan and I have edited a book containing case studies of six urban districts undergoing major reforms to improve academic achievement. Two of the cases, Boston and San Diego, appear most promising, although the outcomes still remain in doubt. See Larry Cuban and Michael Usdan (Eds.), *Powerful Reforms with Shallow Roots* (2002).

7. The recent thrust toward top-down systemic reform driven by mandates and a longing to align state goals, curriculum, textbooks, and assessment first appeared in California during the terms of State Superintendent Bill Honig (1983–1990). For an unusual study of this state effort that focuses on math curricular reform, see Cohen and Hill (2001). Cohen and Hill estimate that 10% of the state's teachers who took advantage of the instructional opportunities to learn how to implement the new math curriculum improved their teaching and, in the researchers' analysis, their students' scores on tests aligned with the new curriculum improved.

District systemic reform, particularly in big cities, mirrors what California and other states have tried. Boston and San Diego are two instances where top-down systemic reform led by superintendents has aimed at building an instructional infrastructure that will help teachers and principals improve teaching and learning. State and district systemic reform is clearly one strategy under way in the early 21st century. There are others. Mayoral control of schools as has happened in Chicago, Boston, Cleveland, and Detroit is another. Superintendents and boards serve at the pleasure of the mayor. Other interventions include state takeovers of districts and sharing of governance of the schools in the hope that state/district partnerships will provide the funds, savvy, and motivation to improve teaching and learning. Baltimore and Philadelphia are examples of such state and district joint ventures. Jim Cibulka and William Boyd nicely point out the strengths and limitations of each of these strategies of changing governance in order to improve students' academic performance. See James Cibulka and William Boyd (Eds.), *A Race Against Time: Responses to the Crisis in Urban Schooling* (in press).

8. Don Schön, *The Reflective Practitioner: How Professionals Think in Action* (1983); F. Elbaz, *Teacher Thinking: A Study of Practical Knowledge* (1983); F. M. Connelly and Diane Clandinin, "Personal Practical Knowledge and the Modes of Knowing: Relevance for Teaching and Learning" in E. Eisner (Ed.), *Learning and Teaching the Ways of Knowing* (1985), pp. 174–198; Lee Shulman, "Knowledge and Teaching: Foundations of the New Reform" (1987), pp. 1–22; K. Carter, "Teachers Knowledge and Learning to Teach" (1990), pp. 291–310; and Gary Fenstermacher, "The Knower and the Known: The Nature of Knowledge in Research on Teaching" (1994), pp. 3–56.

References

Amrein, A. & Berliner, D. (2002). High stakes testing, uncertainty, and student learning. *Education Policy Analysis Archives*, http://epaa.asu.edu/epaa/v10n18/.

Angus, D., Mirel, J., & Vinovskis, M. (1988). Historical development of age stratification in schooling. *Teachers College Record, 90*(2), 213–236.

Archbold, R. (2001, January 14). What makes a good education. *The New York Times*, 27.

Barber, B. (1998). *A passion for democracy*. Princeton, NJ: Princeton University Press.

Becker, H., Ravitz, J., & Wong, YanTien. (1999). Teaching, learning, and computing: 1998 national survey. Center for Research on Information Technology and Organizations, University of California, Irvine and University of Minnesota.

Bennett, N. (1976). *Teaching styles and pupil progress*. Cambridge, MA: Harvard University Press.

Bestor, A. (1953). *Educational wastelands: The retreat from learning in our public schools*. Urbana, IL: University of Illinois Press.

Bok, D. (2001). *The trouble with government*. Cambridge, MA: Harvard University Press.

Bowles, S. & Gintis, H. (1976). *Schooling in capitalist America: Educational reform and the contradictions of economic life*. New York: Basic Books.

Bradley, A. (1993, May 19). The business of reforming Cincinnati's schools. *Education Week*, 1, 16.

Brown v. Board of Education of Topeka, 347 U.S. 483, 493 (1954).

Brown, B. F. (1963).*The nongraded high school*. Englewood Cliffs, NJ: Prentice Hall.

Bullard, P. & Taylor, B. (1993). *Making school reform happen*. Boston: Allyn Bacon.

Callahan, R. (1962). *Education and the cult of efficiency*. Chicago: University of Chicago Press.

Carter, K. (1990). Teachers knowledge and learning to teach. In W. Houston (Ed.), *Handbook of research on teacher education* (pp. 291–310). New York: Macmillan.

Catalyst. (2001,May/June). Mayors in charge.

Chall, J. (1967). *Learning to read: The great debate*. New York: McGraw Hill.

Chaddock, G. (2002, February 26). Mayors, states push school boards aside. *Christian Science Monitor*, 1.

Chubb, J. & Moe, T. (1990). *Politics, markets, and America's schools*. Washington, DC: Brookings Institute.

Cibulka, J. & Boyd, W. (Eds.) (in press). *A race against time: Responses to the crisis in urban schooling*.

Cochran-Smith, M. & Fries, M. (2001). Sticks, stones, and ideology:The discourse of reform in teacher education. *Educational Researcher, 30*(8), 7.

Cohen, D. & Hill, H. (2001). *Learning policy: When state education reform works.* New Haven, CT: Yale University Press.

Coleman, J. (1968). The concept of equality of educational opportunity. *Harvard Educational Review, 38*(1), 7–36.

Connelly, F.M. & Clandinin, D. (1985). Personal practical knowledge and the modes of knowing: Relevance for teaching and learning. In E. Eisner (Ed.), *Learning and teaching the ways of knowing* (pp. 174–198). Chicago: University of Chicago Press.

Consortium for Policy Research in Education. (1998). States and districts and comprehensive school reform. *Policy Briefs,* RB-24.

Counts, G. (1927). *The social composition of boards of education.* Chicago: University of Chicago Press.

Covello, L. (1970). *The heart is the teacher.* Totowa, NJ: Littlefield, Adams & Co.

Cremin, L. (1961). *The transformation of the school.* New York: Vintage.

Cremin, L. (1988). *American education: The metropolitan experience, 1876–1980.* New York: Harper and Brothers.

Cronin, J. (1973). *The control of urban schools.* New York: Free Press.

Cuban, L. (1982). Enduring resiliency: Enacting and implementing federal vocational education legislation. In H. Kantor and D. Tyack (Eds.), *Work, youth, and schooling* (pp. 45–78). Stanford, CA: Stanford University Press.

Cuban, L. (1988). *The managerial imperative and the practice of leadership in schools.* Albany, NY: State University of New York Press.

Cuban, L. (1992). The corporate myth of reforming public schools. *Phi Delta Kappan, 73*(2), 157–159.

Cuban, L. (1993). *How Teachers Taught* (second edition). New York: Teachers College Press.

Cuban, L. (1998). The media and polls on education—Over the years. In G. Maeroff (Ed.), *Imaging education: The media and schools in America* (pp. 69–82). New York: Teachers College Press.

Cuban, L. (2000). Why is it so hard to get "good" schools? In L. Cuban and D. Shipps (Eds.), *Reconstructing the common good: Managing intractable dilemmas* (pp. 148–169). Stanford, CA: Stanford University Press.

Cuban, L. (2001). *How can I fix it? Finding solutions and managing dilemmas—An educators' road map.* New York: Teachers College Press.

Cuban, L. (2001, January 7). The convenient fallacy of education. *San Jose Mercury News,* P1–2.

Cuban, L. (2002). Fast and top-down: Systemic reform and student achievement in San Diego City Schools. In L. Cuban and M. Usdan (Eds.), *Powerful reforms with shallow roots* (pp. 000-000). New York: Teachers College Press.

Cubberley, E. P. (1919). *Public education in the United States.* Cambridge, MA: Riverside.

Curti, M. (1935). *The social ideas of American educators.* Totowa, New Jersey: Littlefield, Adams.

David, J. & Goren, P. (1993).*Transforming education: Overcoming barriers.* Washington, DC: National Governors' Association.

DeGrasse, L. (2001). *Campaign for Fiscal Equity, et. al v. The State of New York, et. al,* 187 Misc.2d1; 719 N.Y.S. 2d 475.

Deschenes, S., Cuban, L., & Tyack, D. (2001). Mismatch: Historical perspectives on schools and students who don't fit them. *Teachers College Record, 103*(4), 525–547.

Dewey, J. (1899). *School and society.* Chicago: University of Chicago.

Dewey, E. & Dewey, J. (1915). *Schools for tomorrow.* New York: E.P. Dutton.

Dewey, J. (1916). *Democracy and education.* New York: Free Press.

Doyle, D. (2000). *The schools we want, the schools we deserve.* Bloomington, IN: Phi Delta Kappa Education Foundation.

Eaton. S. (2002). *The other Boston busing story: What's won and lost across the boundary line.* New Haven, CT: Yale University Press.

Edmonds, R. (1979). Effective schools for the urban poor. *Educational Leadership, 37*(10), 18–24.

Education Week. (1999, January 11). Quality counts 1999, rewarding results, punishing failure.

Education Week. (2001, January 23). Quality counts 2001.

Elam, S. (1989). *The Gallup/Phi Delta Kappa polls of attitudes toward the public schools, 1969–1988.* Bloomington, IN: Phi Delta Kappa.

Elbaz, F. (1983). *Teacher thinking: A study of practical knowledge.* London: Croom Helm.

Elmore, R. & Burney, D. (1998). *Continuous improvement in community district #2, New York City.* Pittsburgh, PA: University of Pittsburgh, Learning Research and Development Center.

Fenstermacher, G. (1994). The knower and the known: The nature of knowledge in research on teaching. *Review of Research in Education, 20,* 3–56.

Finn, C. (1991). *We must take charge: Our schools and our future.* New York: Free Press.

Fones-Wolf, E. (2000). Business propaganda in the schools: Labor's struggle against the Americans for the competitive enterprise system, 1949–1954. *History of Education Quarterly, 40*(3), 255–278.

Fuller, B. (Ed.). (2000). *Inside charter schools: The paradox of radical decentralization.* Cambridge, MA: Harvard University Press.

Gelberg, D. (1997). *The "business" of reforming American schools.* Albany, NY: State University of New York Press.

Goodlad, J. & Anderson, R. (1959). *The nongraded elementary school.* New York: Teachers College Press.

Goodnough, A. (2001, April 9). For Levy, can-do business style runs into education reality. *New York Times,* http://www.nytimes.com/2001/04/09/nyregion/09 Levy.html.

Gorard, S., Fitz, J., & Taylor, C. (2001). School choice impacts: What do we know? *Educational Researcher, 30*(7), 18–23.

Grubb, N. (1997). Dick and Jane at work: The new vocationalism and occupational literacy programs. In G. Hall (Ed.). *Changing work, changing workers* (pp. 159–188). Albany, NY: State University of New York Press.

Gutierrez, R. & Slavin, R. (1992). Achievement effects of the nongraded elementary school: A best evidence synthesis. *Review of Educational Research, 62*(4), 333–376.

Gutmann, A. (1987). *Democratic education.* Princeton, NJ: Princeton University Press.

Hacsi, T. (2002). *Children as pawns: The politics of educational reform.* Cambridge, MA: Harvard University Press.

Handel, M. (2000). Is there a skills crisis? *Public Policy Brief.* No. 62. Annandale-on-Hudson, NY: Bard College, The Jerome Levy Economics Institute.

Hartocollis, A. (2001, November 20). Judge will not allow schools to opt out of regents exams. *The New York Times,* D3.

Hauser, R. (2001). Should we end social promotion? Truth and consequences. In G. Orfield and M. Kornhaber (Eds.), *Raising standards or raising barriers?* (pp. 151–178). New York: The Century Foundation Press.

Hays, C. (1999, May 21). Today's lesson: Soda rights. *The New York Times,* C1, C19.

Heathers, G. (1966). School organization: Nongrading, dual progress, and team teaching. In J. Goodlad (Ed.), *The changing American school* (pp. 110–124). Chicago: National Society for Study of Education.

Hentoff, N. (1966). *Our children are dying.* New York: Viking Press.

Herndon, J. (1968). *The way it spozed to be.* New York: Simon and Schuster.

Hess, F. (1999). *Spinning wheels.* Washington, DC: Brookings Institution.

Hightower, A. (2001). San Diego's big boom: District bureaucracy meets culture of learning. Unpublished doctoral dissertation, Stanford University, Stanford, CA.

Hill, D. (2001, October 10). Breaking up. *Education Week,* 34–39.

Hirsch, E.D. (1995). *The schools that we need and why we don't have them.* New York: Doubleday.

Hogan, D. (1985). *Class and reform: School and society in Chicago, 1880–1930.* Philadelphia: University of Pennsylvania Press.

House, E., Glass, G., McLean, L., & Walker, D. (1978). No simple answer: Critique of the follow through evaluation. *Harvard Educational Review, 48*(2), 128–160.

Jackson, P. (1986). *The practice of teaching.* New York: Teachers College Press.

Jacobson, L. (2001, November 28). Study links income boosts, academic success. *Education Week,* 12.

Jencks, C. (1988). Whom must we treat equally for educational opportunity to be equal. *Ethics, 98*(2), 518–533.

Kahne, J. (1996). *Reframing educational policy: Democracy, community, and the individual.* New York: Teachers College Press.

Kahne, J. & Westheimer, J. (1996). In service of what? The politics of service learning. *Phi Delta Kappan, 77*(9), 592–599.

Kantor, H. (1982). Vocationalism in American education: The economic and political context, 1880–1930. In H. Kantor and D. Tyack (Eds.), *Work, youth, and schooling* (pp. 14–44). Stanford, CA: Stanford University Press.

Kantor, H. (1988). *Learning to earn: School, work, and vocational reform in California, 1880–1930.* Madison, WI: University of Wisconsin Press.

Katz, M. (1968). *The irony of early school reform.* Cambridge, MA: Harvard University Press.

Katznelson, I. & Weir, M. (1985). *Schooling for all: Class, race, and the decline of the democratic ideal.* New York: Basic Books.

Kearns, D. & Doyle, D. (1988). *Winning the brain race: A bold plan to make our schools competitive.* San Francisco, CA: Institute for Contemporary Studies Press.

Kerr, C. (1991, February 7). Is education really that guilty? *Education Week*, p. 30.

Kirp, D. (1995). Changing conceptions of educational equity. In D. Ravitch & M. Vinovskis (Eds.), *Learning from the past* (pp. 97–112). Baltimore: Johns Hopkins University Press.

Kirst, M. & Bulkley, K. (2000). "New, improved" mayors take over city schools. *Phi Delta Kappan, 81*(6), 538–546.

Kliebard, H. (1992). *Forging the American curriculum.* London: Routledge.

Kliebard, H. (1999). *Schooled to work: Vocationalism and the American curriculum, 1876–1946.* New York: Teachers College Press.

Kliebard, H. (1986). *The struggle for the American curriculum, 1893–1958.* Boston: Routledge and Kegan Paul.

Kluger, R. (1976). *Simple justice: The history of* Brown *v.* Board of Education *and black America's struggle for equality.* New York: Knopf.

Kohl, H. (1967). *36 Children.* New York: New American Library.

Kohn, A. (1999, December 9). Tests that cheat students. *New York Times*, A31.

Labaree, D. (1997). Public goods, private goods: The American struggle over educational goals. *American Educational Research Journal, 34*(1), 39–81.

Laboratory of Student Success. (2000). *Achieving student success: A handbook of widely implemented research-based educational reform models.* Philadelphia: Temple University.

Ladd, H. & Hansen, J. (1999). *Making money matter: Financing America's schools.* Washington, DC: National Academy Press.

Lafer, G. (2002). *The job training charade.* Ithaca, NY: Cornell University Press.

Lakoff, G. (1996). *Moral politics: What conservatives know that liberals don't.* Chicago: University of Chicago Press.

Lazerson, M. (1971). *Origins of the urban school: Public education in Massachusetts, 1870–1915.* Cambridge, MA: Harvard University Press.

Lazerson, M. & Grubb, N. (1971). (Eds.) *American education and vocationalism: Documents in vocational education, 1870–1970.* New York: Teachers College Press.

Levin, H. (1998). Educational performance standards and the economy. *Educational Researcher, 27*(4), 4–10.

Lindblom, C. (1977). *Politics and markets: The world's political-economic systems.* New York: Basic Books.

Lips, C. (2000, November). Edupreneurs: A survey of for-profit education. *Policy Analysis, 386.*

Lynd, A. (1953). *Quackery in the public schools.* Boston: Little, Brown.

Marshall, R. & Tucker, M. (1992). *Thinking for a living: Education and the wealth of nations.* New York: Basic Books.

Martin, C. (2000). *Stuck in neutral: The business and politics of human capital investment policy.* Princeton, NJ: Princeton University Press.

Mathews, J. (2001). Chief academic officers. *School Administrator.* http://www.aasa.org/publications/sa/2001_06/mathews_cao.htm.

McClung, M. (2001). Citizenship as the primary purpose of public education. Unpublished paper.

Metz, M. (1990). Real school: A universal drama amid disparate experience. In D. Mitchell and M. Goertz (Eds.), *Education politics for the new century* (pp. 75–91). New York: Falmer.

Meyer, J. & Rowan, B. (1977). Institutionalized organizations: Formal structure as myth and ceremony. *American Journal of Sociology, 83,* 340–363.

Meyer, J. (2000). Reflections on education as transcendence. In L. Cuban and D. Shipps (Eds.), *Reconstructing the common good: Managing intractable dilemmas* (pp. 206–222). Stanford, CA: Stanford University Press.

Mickelson, R. (2000). Corporations and classrooms: A critical examination of the business agenda for urban school reform. In K. McClafferty, C. Torres, and T. Mitchell (Eds.), *Challenges of urban education: Sociological perspectives for the next century* (pp. 127–173). Albany, NY: State University of New York Press.

Mirel, J. (1993). *The rise and fall of an urban school system, Detroit, 1907–1981.* Ann Arbor: The University of Michigan Press.

Molnar, A. (1996). *Giving kids the business: The commercialization of America's schools.* Boulder, CO: Westview.

Molnar, A. & Reaves, J. (2001). *"Buy me! Buy me!" Fourth annual report on trends in schoolhouse commercialism, 2000–2001.* Tempe, AZ: Education Policy Studies Laboratory, Arizona State University.

National Commission on Service-Learning. (2001). *Learning in deed.* Battle Creek, MI: W.W. Kellogg Foundation.

National Education Goals Panel. (1995). *The national education goals report: Building a nation of learners, 1995.* Washington, DC: U. S. Government Printing Office.

Newmann, F. & Wehlage, G. (1995). *Successful school restructuring.* Madison, WI: Center on Organizations and Restructuring.

New York Times on the Web (2001, August 8). Text of Levy's remarks on overhauling staff. http://www.nytimes.com/2001/08/16.

No Child Left Behind. (2002). http://www.ed.gov/offices/OESE/esea/.

Northwest Regional Educational Laboratory. (2001). The catalog of school reform models. http://www.nwrel.org/scpd/catalog/about/shtml.

Oakes, J., Quartz, K., Ryan, S., & Lipton, M. (2000). *Becoming good American schools: The struggle for civic virtue in education reform.* San Francisco: Jossey-Bass.

O'Donnell, M. (2000, September 12). Test prep book for 3rd-graders causes stir. *Chicago Sun Times.*

Orfield, G. & Gordon, N. (2001). Schools more separate: Consequences of a decade of resegregation. Harvard University, Civil Rights Project.

Patterson, J. (2001). Brown v. Board of Education: *A civil rights milestone and its troubled legacy.* New York: Oxford University Press.

Perkinson, H. (1968). *The imperfect panacea: American faith in education, 1865–1965.* New York: Random House.

Perry, N. (1988, November 7). Saving the schools: How business can help. *Fortune,* 42–46, 50–56.

Peterson, P. (1985). *The politics of school reform,* 1870–1940. Chicago: University of Chicago Press.

Petersen, R. (1995). La escuela Fratney. In M. Apple and J. Beane (Eds.), *Democratic schools* (pp. 58–82). Alexandria, VA: Association for Supervision and Curriculum Development.

Pfeffer, J. & Salancik, G. (1978). *External control of organizations.* New York: Harper and Row.

Powell, J.A., Kearney, G., & Kay, V. (2001). *In pursuit of a dream deferred: Linking housing and education policy.* New York: Peter Lang.

Purkey, S. & Smith, M. (1983). Effective schools: A review. *The Elementary School Journal, 83*(4), 427–452.

Putnam, R. (2000). *Bowling alone: The collapse and revival of American community.* New York: Simon and Schuster.

RAND Institute on Education & Training, Policy Brief. (1994). Trial by false fire: Education's role in U.S. "economic decline." No. 4.

Ravitch, D. (1978). *Revisionists revised: A critique of the radical attack on the schools.* New York: Basic Books.

Ravitch, D. (1983). *The troubled crusade.* New York: Basic Books.

Ravitch, D. (2001). *Left back: A century of failed school reforms.* New York: Simon and Schuster.

Rawls, J. (1971). *A theory of justice.* Cambridge, MA: Harvard University Press.

Ray, C. & Mickelson, R. (1990). Business leaders and the politics of school reform. *Politics of education association yearbook, 1989.* London: Taylor and Francis.

Rebell, M. (in press). Education adequacy, democracy, and the courts. In C. Edley, T. Ready, and C. Snow (Eds.) *Achieving high educational standards for all.* Washington, DC: National Academy Press.

Reese, W. (2001). The origins of progressive education. *History of Education Quarterly, 41*(1), 1–24.

Reich, R. (1991). *The work of nations.* New York: Alfred Knopf.

Resnick, L. (2001). The mismeasure of learning. *Education Next, 1*(3), 78–83.

Roemer, J. (1998). *Equality of opportunity.* Cambridge, MA: Harvard University Press.

Rose, L. & Gallup, A. (2000, September). The 32nd annual Phi Delta Kappa/Gallup poll of the public's attitudes toward the public schools. *Phi Delta Kappan, 81*(9), 11.

Rosenbaum, J. (2001). *Beyond college for all.* New York: Russell Sage Foundation.

Rothstein, R. (2002, April 10). An accountability push and fuzzy math. *The New York Times.* A21.

Rothstein, R. (2001, March). The blame game. *The School Administrator.* http://www.aasa.org/publications/sa/2001_03/rothstein.htm.

Rugg, H. & Schumaker, A. (1928). *The child-centered school.* Yonkers-on-the-Hudson, NY: World Publishing.

Ryan, J. (1999). Schools, race, and money. *Yale Law School Journal, 109,* 249–316.

Sanger, D. (2001, January 24). Bush pushes ambitious education plan. *The New York Times,* A1, A14.

Schön, D. (1983). *The reflective practitioner: How professionals think in action.* New York: Basic Books.

Schwartz, W. (1995). Opportunity to learn standards: Their impact on urban students. *ERIC/CUE Digest*, No. 110.

Shanker, A. (1993, May 30). Where we stand. *The New York Times* (paid for by the American Federation of Teachers).

Shepard, L. (1990). The role of assessment in a learning culture. *Educational Researcher, 29*(4), 4–14.

Shepard, L. (2001, January 23–25). *The contest between large-scale accountability testing and assessment in the service of learning: 1970–2001*. Paper prepared for the Spencer Foundation's 30th Anniversary Conference, "Traditions of Scholarship in Education," Chicago, IL.

Shipps, D. (1997). The invisible hand: Big business and Chicago school reform. *Teachers College Record 99*(1), 73–116.

Shipps, D. (1998). Corporate influence on Chicago school reform. In C. Stone (Ed.), *Changing urban education* (pp. 161–183). Lawrence, KN: University of Kansas Press.

Shipps, D. (2000). Echoes of corporate influence: Managing away urban school troubles. In L.Cuban and D. Shipps (Eds.), *Reconstructing the common good in education: Coping with intractable American dilemmas* (pp. 82–106). Stanford, CA: Stanford University Press.

Shulman, L. (1987). Knowledge and teaching: Foundations of the new reform. *Harvard Educational Review, 57*, 1–22.

Sipple, J. (1999). Institutional constraints on business involvement in K–12 education policy. *American Educational Research Journal, 36*(3), 447–488.

Sizer, T. (1984). *Horace's compromise: The dilemma of the American high school*. Boston: Houghton Mifflin.

Smith, E. & Tyler, R. (1942). *Adventures in American education, Vol. III: Appraising and recording student progress*. New York: Harper and Brothers.

Smith, J.P. (1999). Tracking the mathematics of automobile production: Are schools failing to prepare students for work? *American Educational Research Journal, 36*(4), 835–878.

Smith, M. (2000). *American business and political power*. Chicago: University of Chicago Press.

Smith, M. & O'Day, J. (1990). Systemic school reform. In S. Fuhrman and B. Mulen (Eds.), *Politics of education association yearbook* (pp. 233–267). London: Falmer Press.

Smith, R. (1997). *Civic ideals*. New Haven, CT: Yale University Press.

Spring, J. (1975). *Education and the rise of the corporate state*. Boston: Beacon Press.

Strauss, V. (2000, December 26). When success doesn't add up. *Washington Post*, A12.

The Civil Rights Project, Harvard University. (2002). The impact of racial and ethnic diversity on educational outcomes. Cambridge, MA School District.

The National Education Goals Panel. (1995). *The national education goals report: Building a nation of learners*. Washington, DC: U.S. Government Printing Office.

The New York Times Magazine (1991, April 28). p. 21.

The New York Times. (2001, January 30). Text of President Bush's state of the union address to congress, A22.

Thurow, L. (1992). *Head to head: The coming economic battle among Japan, Europe, and America.* New York: Morrow.

Troen, S. (1975). *The public and the schools: Shaping the St. Louis system, 1838–1920.* Columbia, MO: University of Missouri Press.

Tyack, D. (1974). *One best system.* Cambridge, MA: Harvard University Press.

Tyack, D. & Hansot, E. (1982). *Managers of virtue.* New York: Basic Books.

Tyack, D. & Cuban, L. (1995). *Tinkering toward utopia.* Cambridge, MA: Harvard University Press.

U.S. Commission on Excellence in Education. (1983). *A nation at risk.* Washington, DC: U.S. Government Printing Office.

Viadero, D. (2001, November 28). Research: Smaller is better. *Education Week,* 28–30.

Vinovskis, M. (1999). *History of educational policy making.* New Haven, CT: Yale University Press.

Walsh, M. (1999, November 24). Ka-Ching! Business cashing in on learning. *Education Week,* 1, 14–16.

Wells, A. (1993). *Time to choose: America at the crossroads of school choice policy.* New York: Hill and Wang.

Wells, A. & Crain, R. (1994). Perpetuation theory and the long term effects of school desegregation. *Review of Educational Research, 64*(4), 531–555.

Wells, A. & Crain, R. (1997). *Stepping over the color line: African-American students in white suburban schools.* New Haven, CT: Yale University Press.

Westheimer, J. & Kahne, J. (2000). Education for action: Preparing youth for participatory democracy. In W. Ayers & T. Quinn (Eds.), *Democracy and education: A teaching for social justice reader* (pp. 1–20). New York: Teachers College Press.

Wiebe, R. (1962). *Businessmen & reform: A study of the progressive movement.* Cambridge, MA: Harvard University Press.

Wilgoren, J. (2000, August 2). For 2000, the G.O.P. sees education in a new light. *The New York Times,* A15.

Williams et. al. v. State of California et. al. (2000). Superior Court, San Francisco.

Winerip, M. (2001, November 18). Never mind the inventive curriculum. One test fits all. *The New York Times,* A31.

Wirt, F. & Kirst, M. (1997). *The political dynamics of American education.* Berkeley, CA: McCutchan Publishing.

Wolfe, A. (1998). *One nation, after all.* New York: Viking.

Wood, G. (1992). *Schools that work.* Toronto, Canada: Dutton.

Woodring, P. (1953). *Let's talk sense about our schools.* New York: McGraw Hill.

Wrigley, J. (1982). *Class politics and public schools, Chicago 1900– 1950.* New Brunswick, NJ: Rutgers University Press.

Zernike, K. (2000, August 2). Pupils prosper from an investment. *The New York Times,* A11.

Zilversmit, A. (1993). *Changing schools: Progressive education theory and practice, 1930–1960.* Chicago: University of Chicago Press.

Zimmerman, J. (1999). *Distilling democracy: Alcohol education in America's public schools, 1880–1925.* Lawrence, KS: University Press of Kansas.

Index

About the Author

Larry Cuban is Professor Emeritus of Education at Stanford University, Stanford, CA, where he continues to teach courses in the history of school reform, leadership, and policy analysis. He has been faculty sponsor of the Stanford/Schools Collaborative and the Stanford Teachers Education program.

Professor Cuban's background in the field of education prior to becoming a professor includes 14 years of teaching high school social studies in inner-city schools, administering teacher-training programs at schools sites, and serving for 7 years as a district superintendent.

Trained as a historian, Professor Cuban received a B.A. degree from the University of Pittsburgh in 1955 and an M.A. from Cleveland's Case Western University 3 years later. On completing his Ph.D. work at Stanford University in 1974, he became superintendent of the Arlington County (Virginia) public schools, a position he held until he came to Stanford in 1981.

His major research interests focus on the history of curriculum and instruction, educational leadership, school reform, and the different versions of "good" schools, past and present. As a practitioner, he continued to work with teachers and administrators in the Stanford/Schools Collaborative and as a teacher. He has taught courses in U.S. history and economics at two different San Francisco Bay area high schools.

The author of many research and op-ed articles, Professor Cuban has written a number of books, including *How Teachers Taught: Constancy and Change in American Classrooms, 1880–1990* (1993); *Tinkering Toward Utopia* (with David Tyack, 1995); *How Scholars Trumped Teachers: Change without Reform in University Curriculum, Research, and Teaching, 1890–1990* (1999); and *Oversold and Underused: Computers in the Classroom* (2001).